Understand Your Tax Form 1040

Income Taxes Made Easy

Aki Stepinska, EA

First printing, 2022.

This book is published by AkaAki Design.

Cover and interior design by Aki Stepinska

Aki Stepinska, EA
akistepinska@taxguide101.com
Des Plaines, IL, United States of America
www.taxguide101.com

ISBN 978-1-957518-00-8 (ebook)
ISBN 978-1-957518-01-5 (paperback)
ISBN 978-1-957518-02-2 (hardcover)
ISBN 978-1-957518-03-9 (large print)

Disclosure

This book is intended to provide generalized financial information designed to educate a broad segment of the public; it does not give personalized tax, investment, legal, or other business and professional advice.

Before taking any action outlined in this book, you should seek the assistance of a professional who knows your unique situation.

All effort has been made to present accurate, up-to-date, and reliable information. **Tax laws and regulations are complex and subject to change**, which can materially impact investment results. The author cannot guarantee that the information herein is accurate, complete, or timely. **Please verify information with a professional and/or against the IRS regulation.**

By reading this book, the reader agrees that under no circumstances is the author responsible for any losses, direct or indirect, which are incurred due to the use of the information contained within this book, including, but not limited to, — errors, omissions, or inaccuracies.

"Tell me and I forget,
teach me and I may remember,
***involve me** and I learn."*

-Benjamin Franklin

Table of Content

Charts, Tables, Infographics & Other Visuals

ABBREVIATIONS AND ACRONYMS

Below is a list of the most frequently used tax abbreviations and acronyms in the book. In the glossary, located at the end of the book, you can find definitions for many of the terms.

Table 1. Abbreviations and Acronyms

Term	Definition
ACTC	Additional Child Tax Credit
AGI	Adjusted Gross Income
AMT	Alternative Minimum Tax
AOTC	American Opportunity Tax Credit
CDCE	Child and Dependent Care Expenses
COD	Credit for Other Dependents
CTC	Child Tax Credit
DOB	Date of Birth
EA	Enrolled Agent
EIN	Employer Identification Number
EIP	Economic Impact Payment
EITC	Earned Income Tax Credit
ES	Estimated Tax
FUTA	Federal Unemployment Tax
HOH	Head of Household
IP PIN	Identity Protection PIN
IQ	Intelligence Quotient
IRA	Individual Retirement Account
IRS	Internal Revenue Service
IRS FF	IRS Free File
ITIN	Individual Taxpayer Identification Number
MFJ	Married Filing Jointly
MFS	Married Filing Separately
NOL	Net Operating Losses
PEF	Presidential Election Fund
PTC	Premium Tax Credit
QBI	Qualified Business Income
QW	Qualifying Widow(er)
RRC	Rebate Recovery Credit
SSA	Social Security Administration

Term	Definition
SSI	Social Security Income
SSN	Social Security Number
TAC	Taxpayer Assistance Center
TAS	Taxpayer Advocate Service
TCE	Tax Counseling for the Elderly
TCJA	Tax Cuts and Jobs Act
TIN	Taxpayer Identification Number
VITA	Volunteer Income Tax Assistance

"Dear IRS, I am writing to cancel my subscription. Please remove my name from your mailing list."

— Snoopy
by Charles M. Schulz, cartoonist

Introduction

1. About This Book

WHY I Wrote This Book: To Help Taxpayers Understand Their Tax Returns

According to Pew Research, most Americans hate (26%) or dislike (30%) doing their income taxes.[1] One way to change peoples' dislike is to improve their understanding of their tax situation.

There is no lack of tax information. The IRS Title 26 (our individual tax code) is about 6,550 pages long, not including the 60,000 pages of related case law.[2] Hence, for an average taxpayer, tax information is mainly confusing, complicated, and overwhelming.

This book will help you understand Form 1040, which is used to file individual federal income tax returns with the IRS. In addition, it provides you with information on how your refund or tax due is calculated and a big picture view of your taxes.

WHO This Book Is For

This book is for taxpayers who want to understand and learn about their taxes, regardless of their current tax knowledge.

---

[1] *https://www.pewresearch.org/politics/2013/04/11/a-third-of-americans-say-they-like-doing-their-income-taxes/*

[2] *https://www.politifact.com/factchecks/2017/oct/17/roy-blunt/tax-code-so-long-nobodys-really-sure-its-length/*

The **CONVENTIONS** in This Book

❖ All the **visuals** are listed under Tables, Infographics & Figures (TOC).

❖ There are number of **financial and tax terms** used throughout the book. A summary of them is listed under Abbreviations and Acronyms (TOC). In the Glossary under Appendix, you can find definitions of terms used.

❖ **Tables** contain tax summaries, references, and tax information.

❖ **Figures** offer a visual representation of the topic discussed.

❖ **Infographics** simplify textual data in a graphic form.

❖ **Examples** present an actual calculation to help you grasp the concept better. In addition, they help illustrate how taxes are calculated by performing math rather than just talking about it in general terms.

> *Note:* All the examples are hypothetical for illustrative purposes only. All calculations are estimates.

❖ According to **plain language rules, numbers, amounts, and percentages written numerically are easier to grasp**. For that reason, **numbers (1 to 10)** are spelled out just like higher numbers.[3]

---

[3] *https://contented.com/blogs/news/8370188-writing-tip-write-1-2-3-numbers-in-plain-language-and-legal-prose*

❖ **Bold** text highlights important concepts throughout the book. If you want to skim a section, you can scan through the bold text.

❖ *Italic* text distinguishes or emphasizes parts in a section, and provides supplemental information *(parentheses)*.

❖ Underlined text indicates a link to a website. Most links are also provided in footnotes unless they are spelled out as addresses in the body. ***For example***, www.understand1040.com is already a link with a full web address; therefore, it will not be footnoted.

Companion website information. If supplemental information can be found online, it is noted with a computer icon.

❖ Footnotes provide the source of information and are listed at the bottom of each page where referenced. Web addresses are clickable in some eBook formats. For the print readers, the exact web address is provided in the footnote. A shorter archival version is listed for each footnote under www.understand1040.com/resources. Since many website addresses can break (called *Link Rot*[4]) over time, the archival *(permanent)* version preserves the exact copy used. Permanent links have been saved with either perma.cc or archive.st.

[4] *https://harvardlawreview.org/2014/03/perma-scoping-and-addressing-the-problem-of-link-and-reference-rot-in-legal-citations/*

❖ **Forms** listed in under <u>Appendix</u> are visual references and instructions to For 1040 and the three main Schedules. Each box describes the information included. In addition, a source at the bottom of each form links to the most recent IRS copy.

Form 1040: US Individual Income Tax Return

Personal Information.
Spell your name(s) as listed on your SS card(s). Provide the address where you are currently living.

The most important number is your Social Security number (SSN). If you have an Individual Taxpayer Identification Number (ITIN), use that on the SSN line.

Virtual Currency.
Mark "Yes" if you sold, exchanged or received virtual currency in 2021. You don't need to check it if you held it or purchased it.

Filing Status & Requirements (2021).

Status	Income Requirement	Extra over per filer > 65
Single (S)	$12,500	$1,700
Head of Household (HOH)	$18,800	$1,700
Married Filing Jointly (MFJ)	$25,100	$1,350
Qualifying Widow(er) (QW)	$25,100	$1,350
Married Filing Separately (MFS)	$5	

HOH and QW statuses require dependents.

Dependents.
List of child and other dependents who qualified for child tax credit (CTC) or credit for other dependents (COD).

Line 1.
Total wages, salaries, tips, including spouse's income from W-2s.

Line 2a & 2b.
Total tax-exempt interest such as from municipal bonds on 1099-INT or 1099-OID. What's taxable (2b).

Line 3a.
Qualified dividends shown in box 1b of 1099-DIV. Eligible for a lower tax rate when held > 60 days for common stocks.

Line 3b.
Ordinary dividends on 1099-DIV, including REITs. Require Such B if total over $1,500.

Line 4a & 4b.
Total IRA distributions on 1099-R from Roth IRA, traditional IRA, SEP, or SIMPLE IRA. What's taxable (4b).

Line 5a & 5b.
Total pensions & annuities on 1099-R. What's taxable (5b).

Line 6a & 6b.
Total social security benefits on SSA-1099 or RRB-1099. What's taxable (6b).

Line 7.
Capital gain/loss after sell of stocks, investments or home on 1099-DIV, Form 8949 or Sch D.

Line 8.
Additional income from Sch 1 Part I.

Line 9.
Total income.

Line 10.
Adjustments to income (deductions) from Sch 1 Part II.

Line 11.
Adjusted gross income (AGI).

Line 12a.
Itemized (Sch A) or standard deduction (SD).
SD for 2021:
S/MFS - $12,550;
HOH - $18,800;
MFJ/QW - $25,100.

Extra deduction for age over 65 or blindness.

Line 12b.
Charitable deductions up to $300 for S, HOH, QW or MFJ, if you don't itemize.

Line 13.
Qualified Business Income Deduction (QBI) worth up to 20% of business income for qualified business on Sch C or rental on Sch E, calculated on Form 8995.

Line 15.
Taxable income.

Figure 1. Visual Reference & Instruction for Forms

HELP Spread the Word

7 ways to spread the word about this book:

1. Buy a copy of this book.
2. Review the book on Amazon, Goodreads, Barnes & Nobles, or any other favorite book seller.
3. Share your thoughts about it on social media.
4. Sign-up for the author's newsletter on the www.taxguide101.com website.
5. Request the book at your local bookstore.
6. Request the book at your library: Overdrive, New York City, Los Angeles, Chicago, or your city.
7. Share the book on paperbackswap.com, bookcrossing.com, bookmooch.com, or littlefreelibrary.org.

A Special Request

Your brief Amazon review will help others find this book. The link below will take you directly to the Amazon review page.

Thank you in advance. (◠‿◠✿)

https://www.amazon.com/author/akistepinska

Your Feedback

My goal is to have an even better ***Understand Your Tax Form 1040 2.0***, but I can't do that without **your feedback**. Please go to www.understand1040.com and share:

- What did you like (e.g., infographics, cartoons, examples, references, forms, summary tables, quizzes)?
- Which sections did you like the most or would want to expand in the next version?
- What are your tax challenges?
- How did the book help you?
- Did you find an errata (include section, page, and description)?

You can also send feedback directly to akistepinska@taxguide101.com.

2. Qualifications

I have a **BA in Economics and I am an IRS Enrolled Agent (EA).**[5] EA is an IRS designation received after passing a 3-part comprehensive test on individual and business returns. I have worked in international taxation and corporate transfer pricing, a very specialized area of taxation for global multinational companies. Since 2016, I have changed gears and am mainly focused on individual tax.

I have worked at large tax preparation companies as **Master Tax Advisor and Tax Expert**, where I helped taxpayers prepare their tax returns, answer questions, and plan for their future. I have also volunteered with the **IRS Volunteer Income Tax Assistance (VITA)**[6] and the **IRS Tax Counseling for the Elderly (TCE)** programs.

The **Chicago Ladder-up** organization[7] runs the VITA site where I volunteer, and the **AARP Foundation Tax-Aide**[8] runs the TCE site. The IRS-certified programs organize volunteers to prepare tax returns for the elderly and taxpayers in disadvantaged communities.

All the information that I share is honest and to the best of my knowledge. It is important to remember that **each tax situation is unique**. Therefore, you should consult a tax or financial advisor who knows your exact circumstances before making drastic changes.

---

[5] *https://www.irs.gov/tax-professionals/enrolled-agents/enrolled-agent-information*
[6] *https://www.irs.gov/individuals/free-tax-return-preparation-for-qualifying-taxpayers*
[7] *https://www.goladderup.org/our-services/tax-assistance/*
[8] *https://www.aarp.org/money/taxes/aarp_taxaide/*

3. Companion Websites

The tax world is frequently changing. Therefore, some of the information in the book may need to be updated, and thus the companion websites at www.taxguide101.com and www.understand1040.com/resources.

The websites will contain many additional resources and bonuses, that are currently being developed *(coming)*, such as:

- List of all the **sources** used together with **permanent archival links**.
- Other **suggested content** and articles.
- Sign-up for a ***Tax Tips* Newsletter**.
- **Excel files** of the examples and calculations presented in the book which you can download for free or extra charge and update with your information *(coming)*.
- Link to **YouTube videos** *(coming)*.
- Link to an **Online Tax Course** *(coming)*.
- **Pdfs**, **Quizzes**, surveys, merchandise.
- Additional **charts**, examples, **presentations**, and resources not published in the book.
- Link to connect with me on **social media**.
- **Corrections**.

Thank you! (^◡^)っ ♡

Taxpayer Challenges

TAXPAYER CHALLENGES

Everyone makes mistakes, but some mistakes, especially **tax mistakes, can be costly**. Minor negligence can lead to a full-blown audit. Nevertheless, only between 0.5 to 0.6 taxpayers get audited each year,[9] so the likelihood is small. **The best preventive measure you can take is to avoid tax mistakes in the first place.**

---

[9] *Depending which year you review it can be between 1 in 200 (2017) to 1 in 166 (2018) or less. https://www.nolo.com/legal-encyclopedia/what-are-the-odds-being-audited.html*

Even if you receive a letter from the IRS, understand that Uncle Sam sends millions of letters each year to the taxpayers for many reasons. You could receive a letter because:

- You have a balance due;
- You are due a larger or smaller refund;
- IRS has a question about your tax return;
- IRS needs to verify your identity;
- IRS requires additional information;
- IRS made changes to your return;
- IRS needs to notify you of delays in processing your return.

When you receive a letter from the IRS, take a deep breath, read it carefully and read the instructions on what you need to do.

Taxpayers face many challenges when dealing with taxes and the IRS. **Two taxpayers' challenges** are listed below,[10] with an estimated number of affected individuals. Many of the issues are discussed in **the 2019 Annual Report to Congress**[11] **published by the Taxpayer Advocate Service (TAS).**

---

[10] *https://www.irsmind.com/audits/top-6-tax-problems-encountered-by-taxpayers/*

[11] *https://www.taxpayeradvocate.irs.gov/wp-content/uploads/2020/08/ARC19_Volume1.pdf*

157 MILLION OVERCOMPLICATED TAX CODE.

Each year there are major or minor tax law changes. Since 2001, there have been more than 3,250 changes to the tax code, which is thousands of pages long. Since 1975, the number of words in the code tripled.[12] As a result, **an overcomplicated tax code makes compliance difficult** for all taxpayers.

For example, the code has many temporary provisions that repeatedly expire and then get extended. On top of that, determinations for all provisions are not consistent.

For example, the definition of a dependent varies widely across deductions and credits. In addition, there are various phase-out limits for many tax breaks.

For example, the maximum phase-out limits[13] for MFJ varies across different deductions and credits, as shown in **Table 2** below.

---

[12] *https://www.irs.gov/pub/tas/08_tas_arc_msp_1.pdf*

[13] *Phase-out is the amount of MAGI or AGI, or any other specified amount of income at which point the amount of credit is either limited or no longer available to taxpayers.*

Table 2. Various Deductions & Credit Max Phase-outs for MFJ (2021)

Roth IRA deduction:	$208,000
Traditional IRA deduction *(with contributing spouse coverage)*:	$125,000
Student Loan Interest deduction:	$170,000
American Opportunity credit:	$180,000
Child and Dependent Care credit:	$440,000
Earned Income Tax Credit:	$57,414 (3+ children)
Economic Impact Payments:	$198,000 (EIP1); $174,000 (EIP2); $160,000 (EIP3);

There were 157 million tax returns filed for the tax year 2019.[14] Taxpayer burden for the tax year 2018 was 7.9 billion hours for record keeping, learning about the law, and filing tax returns, which was equivalent to $271 billion in opportunity cost lost.[15]

About 52% of taxpayers paid someone else to prepare their taxes,[16] equal to $97 billion out-of-pocket costs. The tax preparation industry employs 3.8 million full-time workers. Even if you decide to hire someone to help you file your taxes, you should have a basic understanding of your tax Form 1040.

---

[14] *pg. 4: https://www.irs.gov/pub/irs-pdf/p55b.pdf*

[15] *Calculated by taking the 7.854 billions of hours times the US average of $34.72 per hour worked on non-federal civilian employee compensation in Dec 2019. https://www.ntu.org/foundation/detail/tax-complexity-2020-compliance-burdens-ease-for-second-year-since-tax-reform*

[16] *For 2019 tax season 80.6 million used tax preparer out of 153.7 million tax returns processed. https://www.efile.com/efile-tax-return-direct-deposit-statistics/*

77 MILLION **LACK OF TAX KNOWLEDGE.**

Taxpayers who miss deductions and credits overpay on taxes. If you have don't understand your taxes or use an inexperienced tax preparer, you lose on getting all the tax breaks you qualify for. That is why 52% of taxpayers pay someone to get their taxes done.[17]

Even if taxpayers are familiar with few benefits, they often don't grasp all the differences and advantages. **For example**, taxpayers who understand one retirement plan don't necessarily know all the qualifications or benefits between the traditional IRA, Roth IRA, SEP IRA, 401(k) plans, etc.[18] There is a strong link between taxpayer knowledge and understanding, and tax compliance.[19] If you are not clear about all the rules and subtlety of the tax code, it is hard to comply fully.

The very wealthy have sophisticated teams of professionals that help them find loopholes and eliminate their tax liabilities. While the average taxpayers, who want to take advantage of the tax code, can make inadvertent errors, leading to IRS penalties or an audit. The tax system works differently for taxpayers in the top vs. the bottom tax brackets.

Average taxpayers have minimal tax understanding. According to NerdWallet, 46% to 58% of individuals don't

---

[17] *pg. 56: https://www.taxpayeradvocate.irs.gov/wp-content/uploads/2020/08/ARC19_Volume1.pdf*
[18] *https://www.irs.gov/pub/tas/08_tas_arc_msp_1.pdf*
[19] *http://download.garuda.ristekdikti.go.id/article.php?article=1031092&val=11484&title=Why%20is%20Tax%20Knowledge%20and%20Tax%20Understanding%20Important*

understand basic tax concepts.[20] In addition, the Journal of Consumer Policy observed that 30% to 79% of consumers have significant gaps in essential tax knowledge.[21]

As of 2020 Census data, in the United States, there were 258.3 million adults.[22] Based on the percentages of individuals with low tax understanding, conservatively speaking, more than 77 million[23] adults lack basic tax knowledge. This book is trying to change that, one taxpayer at a time. We are starting with the basic understanding of our tax Form 1040. In the next book, Boost Your Tax IQ, I will cover most topics for an average filer in more detail.

[20] *https://www.nerdwallet.com/article/taxes/americans-dont-know-much-about-taxes-or-that-they-might-get-them-done-for-free*

[21] *https://link.springer.com/article/10.1007/s10603-020-09460-2*

[22] *https://www.census.gov/library/stories/2021/08/united-states-adult-population-grew-faster-than-nations-total-population-from-2010-to-2020.html*

[23] *This is a conservative range of 30% times the total adult population of 258.3 million (258.3 mil x 30% = 77 mil). The most aggressive estimate would be based on 79% of taxpayers not understanding taxes, which would equal to 204 million (258.3 mil x 79% = 204 mil). The main point is that many taxpayers don't understand the complex tax code and miss out on all the benefits.*

Behavioral Insight for Tax Compliance

First of all, give yourself a break. To be good at doing and understanding your taxes, you have to know few things about *human nature* and fight against it. **Behavioral Insight** analyzes how people think and behave by studying psychology, neuroscience, and behavioral economics.[24]

Below are just a few ingrained habits that we have to face while doing taxes:

- **Daily we are faced with more decisions and information than we can consciously process.** We have two ways of processing information: 1) fast or 2) slow. Most of the information we process is done fast without a lot of conscious thought. Slow processing is deliberate, requires more of our mental resources, and is harder. **For example**, tasks at the end of a very long tax form or tax appointment may be less accurate and complete because your energy has already been depleted. Therefore, it may be better for you to review and prepare your taxes not in one sitting but over a couple of days so you can break challenging sections into shorter segments.

- **When we face challenges**, tedious tasks and stress, we often become drained, which **leads to sub-optimal decision-making and shortcuts**. We make choices that may not be best for us and our future. Like instead of reviewing a very long tax form or searching our home for additional documentation, we fall for a quick option.

[24] *https://www.irs.gov/pub/irs-soi/17rpirsbehavioralinsights.pdf*

❖ **We are influenced by first and easy choices** than succeeding and more challenging options. Tax forms that list sub-optimal options at the top or as default can disadvantage taxpayers with a limited understanding and time.

❖ **We don't feel the same when we sign tax information electronically.** The responsibility and commitment feels less serious and real than signing paper documents. However, tax returns are legal documents that you sign under penalties of perjury.

Tax Info and Forms

From the get-go, taxes are complicated. They can be confusing, full of exceptions and contradictions, non-common-sense definitions, and references to many other rules and regulations. If you are exposed to taxes only once a year, everything you learn during your filing is easily forgotten until the following year.

Forms

There are almost 800 IRS Forms and instructions[25] that the agency publishes on its website. IRS website also has a list of almost 120 publications and guides[26] on variety of tax topics. The agency provides access to information but does not guarantee that it is clear.

For example, for some forms, the instructions state that to determine whether you need to file them, you first need to complete them. On top of that, many forms and schedules are interlinked. **For example**, form one may require information from couple other forms that eventually flow into a schedule. As a result, keeping track of what is going on and preventing mistakes is hard from the start.

Definitions

Tax code terms don't follow common-sense everyday usage, which creates confusion for taxpayers. **For example**,

---

[25] *https://www.theatlantic.com/ideas/archive/2019/04/american-tax-returns-dont-need-be-painful/586369/*
[26] *https://www.irs.gov/publications*

the definition of a "qualifying child" is different when claiming EITC, CTC, or other benefits.[27]

Some definitions rather than define the tax item itself define what it is NOT, such as with capital asset.[28] Over time, per case laws and additional IRS regulations, the definition becomes clarified. However, there is a lag between when the tax term was used and when it is defined.

Code

The tax code is between 2,600 and 70,000 pages long. Why such a discrepancy? Some organizations count all the supporting IRS regulations and revenue rulings, which explain how to apply the tax code, as part of it.[29] Regardless of how you see it, the tax code is very long and not written in plain English.

Exceptions

Another obstacle to a clear tax code is the number of exceptions. Even if you have a good understanding of general tax rules, you may not be aware of several exceptions, which can impact tax returns in significant ways.

For example, if you look at the rules for claiming a dependent, which is a frequent tax concept, there are 4 exceptions listed. The summary table for the definition is also meant as an overview of the general rules for a

---

[27] *https://www.brookings.edu/testimonies/tax-simplification-issues-and-options/*
[28] *https://www.law.cornell.edu/uscode/text/26/1221*
[29] *https://irisreading.com/how-long-would-it-take-to-read-the-entire-u-s-tax-code/*

dependent. For details, you have to review publication 501, which is 29 pages long.[30]

Table 5. **Overview of the Rules for Claiming a Dependent**

CAUTION *This table is only an overview of the rules. For details, see the rest of this publication.*

- You can't claim any dependents if you, or your spouse if filing jointly, could be claimed as a dependent by another taxpayer.
- You can't claim a married person who files a joint return as a dependent unless that joint return is filed only to claim a refund of withheld income tax or estimated tax paid.
- You can't claim a person as a dependent unless that person is a U.S. citizen, U.S. resident alien, U.S. national, or a resident of Canada or Mexico.[1]
- You can't claim a person as a dependent unless that person is your **qualifying child** or **qualifying relative.**

Tests To Be a Qualifying Child	**Tests To Be a Qualifying Relative**
1. The child must be your son, daughter, stepchild, foster child, brother, sister, half brother, half sister, stepbrother, stepsister, or a descendant of any of them.	1. The person can't be your qualifying child or the qualifying child of any other taxpayer.
2. The child must be (a) under age 19 at the end of the year and younger than you (or your spouse if filing jointly), (b) under age 24 at the end of the year, a student, and younger than you (or your spouse if filing jointly), or (c) any age if permanently and totally disabled.	2. The person either (a) must be related to you in one of the ways listed under *Relatives who don't have to live with you*, or (b) must live with you all year as a member of your household[2] (and your relationship must not violate local law).
3. The child must have lived with you for more than half of the year.[2]	3. The person's gross income for the year must be less than $4,300.[3]
4. The child must not have provided more than half of his or her own support for the year.	4. You must provide more than half of the person's total support for the year.[4]
5. The child must not be filing a joint return for the year (unless that joint return is filed only to claim a refund of withheld income tax or estimated tax paid).	
If the child meets the rules to be a qualifying child of more than one person, generally only one person can actually treat the child as a qualifying child. See *Qualifying Child of More Than One Person*, later, to find out which person is the person entitled to claim the child as a qualifying child.	

[1] There is an exception for certain adopted children.

[2] There are exceptions for temporary absences, children who were born or died during the year, children of divorced or separated parents (or parents who live apart), and kidnapped children.

[3] There is an exception if the person is disabled and has income from a sheltered workshop.

[4] There are exceptions for multiple support agreements, children of divorced or separated parents (or parents who live apart), and kidnapped children.

Figure 2. Exceptions to Claiming a Dependent

[30] *Pub 501 "Dependents, Standard Deduction, and Filing Information" (pg 5): https://www.irs.gov/pub/irs-pdf/p501.pdf*

ALL ABOUT 1040

The U.S. taxpayers use Form 1040 to file their federal income tax returns. This form is used to file personal taxes.

On the form:

- You report the amount of income received during the tax year
- Calculate how much of it is taxable
- List how much you have already pre-paid during the year
- Claim credits and deductions
- Calculate your refund or how much you owe.

WHAT IS TAX FORM 1040

The 1040 Form is **divided into sections and has step-by-step calculations** of how much you will owe in taxes or how big your refund will be. If you are like 90% of taxpayers and are filing electronically,[31] you may not even realize which section of 1040 you are working on until you see a printed copy.

That is one reason why taxpayers are unclear how to read their 1040. When filing your taxes with a tax preparer or using tax software, you never go through the preparation process the same way that 1040 is organized.

In a perfect world, we would calculate our tax simply like this:

(Income - Deductions) * Tax Rate = **Tax**

Tax - Credits = **Total Tax**

Total Tax - Payments = **Refund or Amount Due**

However, since we are dealing with tax calculations, the **computations are anything but simple**. Several categories are added and subtracted on the 1040 form multiple times.

---

[31] *Table A: Total filers of 157 million in 2019, 142 filed electronically. https://www.irs.gov/pub/irs-pdf/p1304.pdf*

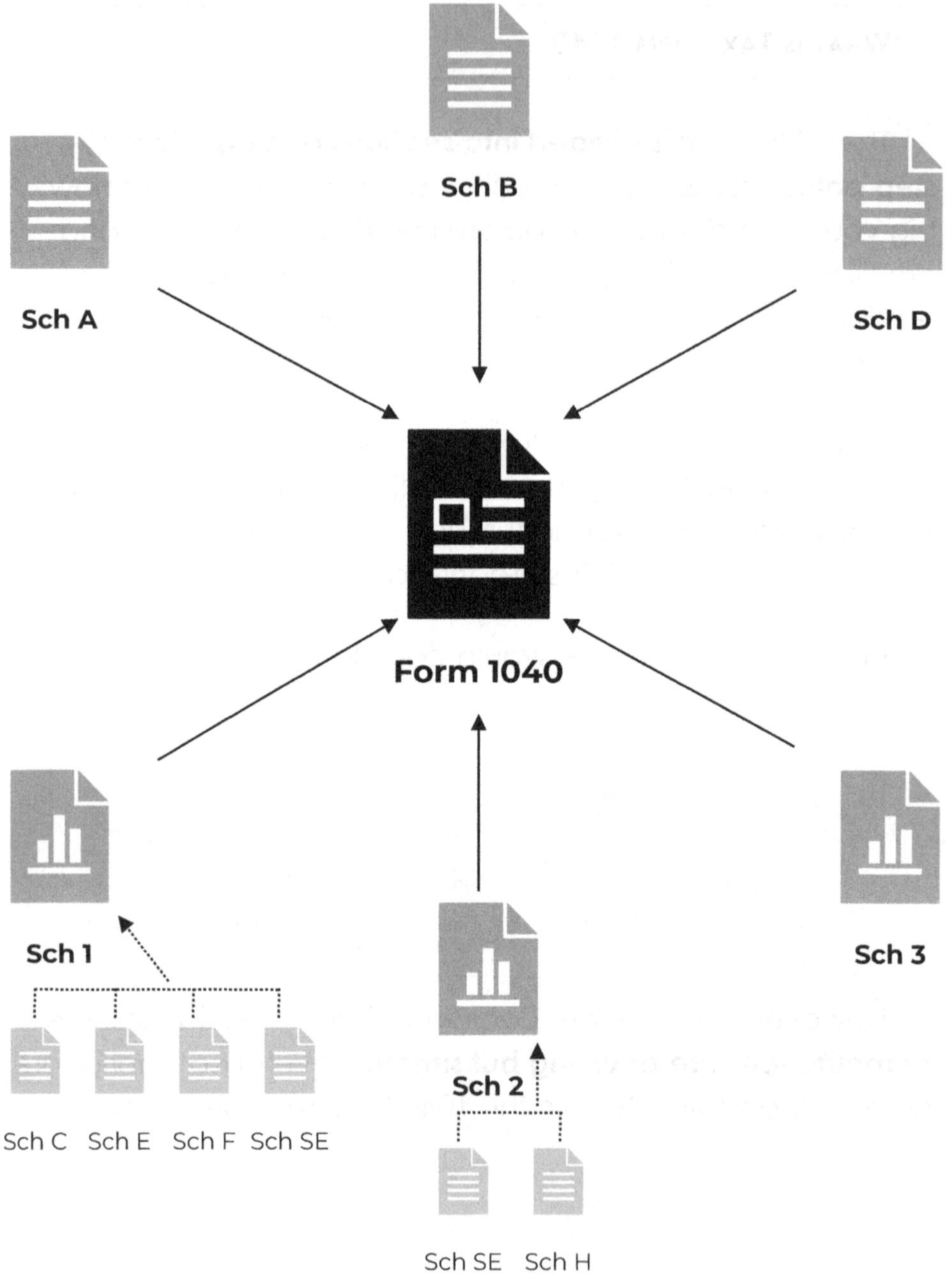

Figure 3. Form 1040 & Other Schedules

There are several reasons for the numerous entries. First, **different income is taxed at varying tax rates** *(e.g., wages (Form 1040 line (L1) vs. capital gain(L7))*. Second, **non-refundable credits** can reduce your tax liability only to zero *(e.g., foreign tax credit (L20))*. In contrast, **refundable credits** *(e.g., EITC, AOTC, RRC (L27-30))* can lead to a refund even if you have zero tax liability. Finally, taxes outside the 1040 form must be added to your tax due amount *(e.g., self-employment taxes (L23))*.

Form 1040 is **two pages long, but it references several other forms and schedules** *(see **Figure 3** below)*. For example, there are **three main schedules**, split into two parts each, listed six times on 1040, which can be difficult to follow. Furthermore, the three schedules are not even listed in a consecutive order *(Sch 3, Part I before Sch 2, Part II)*. That may make sense to the IRS but not to most taxpayers.

Schedule 1 includes **income** not directly listed on 1040 such as alimony, business income *(Sch C)*, rental income *(Sch E)*, farm income *(Sch F)*, and unemployment income. As you notice, each of these incomes has more schedules that need to be completed and flow into Schedule 1.

Schedule 1 also covers **deductions** *(subtractions)* from income such as:

- educator expenses
- military moving expenses
- HSA deduction
- IRA deduction
- student loan interest
- self-employment health insurance
- half of self-employment tax
- deductible retirement contributions
- and others

Schedule 2 includes **all types of taxes** that need to be added to your tax due:

- AMT
- Excess advanced premium tax credit repayment
- Self-employment tax
- Extra taxes on IRAs
- Household employment taxes
- Repayment of the first-time homebuyer credit
- Additional Medicare tax
- Net investment tax

Schedule 3 includes all types of **credits and payments** made. These reduce the amount of tax due. *For example*, non-refundable credits can reduce your tax amount to zero but not below. In contrast, payments and refundable credits can bring your tax liability below zero and lead to a refund.

Non-refundable Credits (Sch 3, Part I):

- foreign tax credit
- non-refundable part of the credit for child and dependent care expenses.
- non-refundable education credits
- retirement savings contribution credit
- adoption credit
- credit for elderly or disabled
- alternative motor vehicle credits.

Payments and refundable Credits (Sch 3, Part II):

- net premium tax credit
- payments made with extension to file
- qualified sick and family leave
- refundable part of the credit for child and dependent care expenses.

The information from the three schedules flows into Form 1040. Additionally, so does information from many other Forms *(8995, 8863, etc.)* and Schedules *(A, D, EITC, etc.)*. You only attach forms and schedules to your 1040 if they are used.

Table 3. 1040 Schedules

Sch 1, Part I	- additional **income** *(addition)*
Sch 1, Party II	- **deductions** *(subtraction from income)*
Sch 2, Part I	- other **taxes** *(addition to tax due)*
Sch 2, Part II	- additional **taxes** *(addition to tax due)*
Sch 3, Part I	- other **non-refundable credits** that can reduce the tax liability to zero *(subtractions from tax)*
Sch 3, Part II	- additional **refundable credits** that can reduce tax liability below zero and lead to a refund *(subtractions from tax)*
Sch A	- used to list all **itemized deductions** such as medical, mortgage interest, state and local taxes, charitable donations, etc.
Sch B	- reports **interest & dividend income** above $,1,500
Sch C	- reports profit or loss from **self-employment**
Sch D	- used to report **capital gains or losses** from investments, sale of stocks, property or real estate
Sch E	- income or loss from **rental real estate**, royalties, partnerships, S-corps, estates, trusts, and other pass-through entities
Sch F	- reports income or loss from **farming**
Sch H	- used to report SS and Medicare taxes paid for **household workers** such as nanny or maid
Sch J	- used by farmers & fishermen for 3-year tax averaging
Sch R	- used to claim the senior or disability tax credit
Sch SE	- used to calculate **self-employment tax** on net profit over $400

Form 1040 had a significant overhaul after passing the **Tax Cuts and Jobs Act (TCJA)** in 2018 but even since then it has changed each year. For the tax year 2021, it contains a reference to 7 schedules and 7 forms and the taxpayers are asked to "see instructions" 15 times (see Appendix: Forms & Schedules).

The tax Form 1040 is constantly changing, and each year it has some modifications. ***For example***, below are a few changes for the past two years.

The **tax year 2020 version** of Form 1040:

- Had a question added asking each taxpayer whether at any time during the year they received, sold, sent, exchanged, or acquired financial interests in any virtual currency.[32]
- Allowed taxpayers with standard deductions to deduct charitable contributions up to $300 per return.
- Included Recovery Rebate Credit to reconcile the taxpayers' amount of stimulus payments.

The **tax year 2021 version** of Form 1040:[33]

- Moved the charitable contributions for taxpayers with standard deductions after AGI.
- Added three additional EITC subsections.
- Expanded many items on the 1040 Schedules 1-3.

---

32 *https://www.cnbc.com/2021/02/24/failure-to-report-crypto-on-tax-returns-can-lead-to-trouble-with-irs.html*

33 *Final version as of Dec 2021. https://www.irs.gov/pub/irs-pdf/f1040.pdf*

You can see the complexity of taxes first hand just by examining the **Form 1040 instructions which are 115 pages long**[34] and:

- reference other forms (480) and schedules (273) many times;
- mention additional "worksheets" 135 times;
- list exceptions 44 times;
- ask you to add (39), subtract (62), multiply (25), and divide (4) *(and you thought elementary math was over)*;
- compare things that are smaller (22), larger (6), or ask you to combine items (9).

No wonder we need help completing our taxes. It can get overwhelming for most taxpayers. At one point, there were discussions about making Form 1040 the size of a postcard. However, without simplifying the tax code, that only leads to the calculations being done on additional schedules and forms that are added as attachments.

In addition to the instructions for Form 1040, the IRS publishes annually a supplemental document called **Publication 17.**[35] It is a handy guide for individual taxpayers explaining the income tax law in a clearer and more taxpayer-friendly language than the Form 1040 instructions.

---

[34] *https://www.irs.gov/pub/irs-pdf/i1040gi.pdf*
[35] *https://www.irs.gov/forms-pubs/about-publication-17*

The **complex layout**, unfamiliar terms, and the many choices that taxpayers need to analyze, make preparing taxes very challenging *(see* The Behavioral Insights for Tax Compliance *on how our natural habits make preparing taxes a challenge)*. However, we have to work with what we have, at least for the time being.

Cartoon 1 - 1040 Chaos Theory

DIFFERENT TYPES OF 1040S

Taxpayers who are U.S. residents and citizens have to file their personal federal taxes with the IRS on **Form 1040**. The form reports your gross income, how much of it is taxable, what are your tax deductions and credits, and whether you should receive a refund or have tax due for the year.

Another version of Form 1040 made an entrance with the passing of TCJA. **Form 1040-SR** was specifically designed for seniors. It gives greater prominence to **retirement benefits**.[36] The main differences between 1040 and 1040-SR are the cosmetics such as **larger font**, no shading, accessible color scheme, and embedded standard deduction table.

On the other hand, Form **1040-NR**[37] is required to be completed by taxpayers who:[38]

- are non-resident aliens and are engaged in a trade or business in the U.S. or
- have the U.S. sourced income and didn't have enough in withholdings.

Taxpayers located in U.S. territories and possessions and who have more than **$400 in net self-employment income** must complete **Form 1040-SS.**[39] The U.S. territories include Guam, American Samoa, the U.S. Virgin Islands, Puerto Rico, and the Northern Mariana Islands. Form **1040-PR** is a Spanish

---

[36] *https://www.investopedia.com/taxes/seniors-get-new-simplified-tax-form/*
[37] *https://www.irs.gov/pub/irs-pdf/f1040nr.pdf*
[38] *https://1040abroad.com/blog/who-needs-to-file-form-1040nr-nonresident-alien-tax-return/*
[39] *https://www.irs.gov/pub/irs-pdf/i1040ss.pdf*

version of the 1040-SS form for the self-employed taxpayers in Puerto Rico.

Before the TCJA, there were also Forms 1040-EZ and 1040-A. **These forms have been retired** starting with the tax year 2018. Form 1040-EZ was used for the most straightforward tax returns, primarily for taxpayers with W-2 income less than $100,000 without dependents. Form 1040-A[40] was used by taxpayers who earned less than $100,000 and didn't itemize their taxes.

Another version of 1040 that is used by over 3 million[41] taxpayers each year is Form 1040-X.[42] It is filed by taxpayers who want to **amend tax returns** that they previously filed. The form should not be used to fix mathematical errors[43] but rather **complete material changes**. Starting with the tax year 2019, Form 1040-X became electronically available, which reduced the complexity and hassle of filing an amendment. The form contains information on the initially filed information, what changed, and the final calculations.

Two other versions of Form 1040 are essential to note, although not many people think of them as forms but rather **payment vouchers**. Form 1040-ES[44] is used to figure out and **pay estimated taxes**. It is often generated by tax preparation software to help taxpayers figure out how much in estimated payments they need to make to avoid the underpayment

---

[40] *https://www.investopedia.com/terms/1/1040a.asp*

[41] *https://www.irs.gov/newsroom/now-available-irs-form-1040-x-electronic-filing*

[42] *https://www.irs.gov/forms-pubs/about-form-1040x*

[43] *The IRS fixes mathematical errors, and the taxpayer will receive a CP11, CP12, or CP13 notices.*

[44] *https://www.irs.gov/forms-pubs/about-form-1040-es*

penalty. If taxpayers pay their quarterly taxes electronically, the form doesn't even have to be used.

Form 1040-V[45] is a payment voucher taxpayers send with check or money order to the IRS for any Form 1040 or 1040-NR balance due.

We will only focus on Form 1040, which U.S. taxpayers primarily use. If you get to know that form, you will understand all the other versions. See **Table 4** below for description of all Form 1040s.[46]

[45] *https://www.irs.gov/forms-pubs/about-form-1040-v*
[46] *https://www.investopedia.com/terms/1/1040.asp*

Table 4. Different Form 1040s

Form	Detail
1040	**Standard** IRS form for US individuals filing federal taxes.
1040-SR	Introduced for tax year 2018 for **seniors**. It has a larger font and no shading. Retirement benefits receive greater prominence.
1040-NR	A version for **nonresident aliens**. It is the longest version of 1040.
1040-SS	A version for residents of **US territories** such as American Samoa, the CNMI, Guam, Puerto Rico, and the US Virgin Islands with net-self employment income and who don't have to file Form 1040.
1040-PR	A **Spanish version** of Form 1040-SS.
1040-ES	This form is used to pay **estimated quarterly taxes** for income that isn't subject to withholding, such as self-employment, interest, dividends, and rents.
1040-V	A short **payment voucher** that accompanies payment for any balance on Form 1040 or 1040-NR.
1040-X	A version to file any changes and **amendment** to a previously filed 1040.
1040-EZ	A version used for simpler returns, those primarily with W-2 income. **Retired in tax year 2018.**
1040-A	A version used by taxpayers who made less than $100,000 and didn't itemize. **Retired in tax year 2018.**

How to Get a 1040 Form

There are several ways to obtain a copy of Form 1040. First, if you are using tax software, the form will be generated for you automatically. If you would like to download a pdf version of the form, you can obtain it from the IRS website.[47]

The Form 1040 for the tax year 2021, which is used in the book, became finalized and available in mid-December of 2021.[48] The IRS usually doesn't start processing tax returns until early February (for the tax year 2020, it began processing returns on Feb 12, 2021). So if Congress makes any last-minute changes in early January, the IRS still has time to update the form. However, the most likely scenario is changes to the schedules rather than Form 1040 itself.

You have a few options if you want a paper copy of the form but cannot print it yourself. First, many libraries have copies of the federal and state tax forms, together with instructions, so check with **your local library**.[49]

You can also obtain tax forms from the **Taxpayer Assistance Centers (TAC)**.[50] In the past, taxpayers could stop by at TAC at any time. However, since the Coronavirus pandemic, taxpayers are asked to make an appointment before coming.

---

[47] *https://www.irs.gov/pub/irs-pdf/f1040.pdf*

[48] *However, the Form 1040 instructions were not available as of the publishing date of this book.*

[49] *https://www.careeronestop.org/LocalHelp/CommunityServices/find-libraries.aspx*

[50] *https://www.irs.gov/help/contact-your-local-irs-office*

You can also request to **receive tax forms by mail by calling 1-800-TAX-FORM** (1-800-829-3676) or via **the IRS website.**[51] In addition, for taxpayers with disabilities, the 1040 form is available in Braille or plain text version.[52]

[51] *https://www.irs.gov/forms-pubs/forms-and-publications-by-us-mail*
[52] *https://www.irs.gov/forms-pubs/irs-tax-forms-in-braille-and-text-formats*

When to File Form 1040

Each tax season **starts around mid-February** and lasts until April 15. If the IRS issues a new tax form before mid-February, you can prepare it and submit it, but the IRS won't start processing it until mid-February.[53]

According to the IRS Section 6072(a) code, **the tax due date is April 15**.[54] However, for the past three years, the tax due date has not been April 15.

For the tax year 2021, because April 15 falls on Good Friday, **the tax due date is April 18, 2022**. For the tax year 2019, the due date was July 15, 2020, while for the tax year 2020, the due date was prolonged until May 17, 2021. Both years had extended due dates because of the Covid-19 pandemic.

If you cannot file your tax return by April 15, you can request a **six-month extension** (Form 4868)[55] which gives you until October 15 of the year to file. The extension gives you more time to file but not more time to pay. If you don't submit any payment at the original tax due date and owe, you may be charged interest and penalties.

---

[53] *https://www.irs.gov/newsroom/2021-tax-filing-season-begins-feb-12-irs-outlines-steps-to-speed-refunds-during-pandemic*
[54] *https://www.irs.gov/pub/irs-drop/n-11-17.pdf*
[55] *https://www.irs.gov/pub/irs-pdf/f4868.pdf*

The statute of limitation on refunds is 3 years from the deadline or 2 years from the date you paid taxes.[56] It means that after that time, you won't be able to get a refund, and the unclaimed money will go to the U.S. Treasury. During tax season 2022, **taxpayers can still claim the 2018 tax return refunds**. However, it is always best to file your taxes in the current year because you have electronic filing options.

When you file prior year taxes, you can only do so via paper. Tax software companies do offer software for previous years, but it can be expensive. An alternative option is to visit a **Volunteer Income Tax Assistance (VITA) site**[57] and have the volunteers prepare your prior-year tax returns for free and then mail it out yourself.

---

[56] *https://www.thebalance.com/irs-statute-of-limitations-3192947*
[57] *https://www.irs.gov/individuals/free-tax-return-preparation-for-qualifying-taxpayers*

WHERE TO SEND YOUR FORM 1040

If you are electronically filing, which is the most efficient way to file, you don't have to worry about mailing your Form 1040 to the right address. However, if you are paper filing, you must double-check you are sending it to the correct IRS site. Otherwise, the processing of your tax return could be delayed. Under a section titled ***"Where Do You File?"*** in the Form 1040 instruction,[58] there is a list of 14 addresses to choose from *(see **Figure 4**)*.

The address where you send your paper return depends on where you live and whether you include a payment. The address you send your tax return to can also be contingent on when you are mailing it *(as it was for tax year 2020)*. It is important to double-check the address for the current tax year as they do change.

As a result, taxpayers have many opportunities to make mistakes when they are paper filing. **Electronic filing is not only easier but also ensures the IRS receives your tax returns.**

[58] *End of 1040 instruction: https://www.irs.gov/pub/irs-pdf/i1040gi.pdf*

IF you live in...	THEN use this address if you: Are requesting a refund or are not enclosing a check or money order...	Are enclosing a check or money order...
Alabama, Georgia, North Carolina, South Carolina, Tennessee	Department of the Treasury Internal Revenue Service Kansas City, MO 64999-0002	Internal Revenue Service P.O. Box 1214 Charlotte, NC 28201-1214
Alaska, California, Colorado, Hawaii, Idaho, Kansas, Michigan, Montana, Nebraska, Nevada, North Dakota, Ohio, Oregon, South Dakota, Utah, Washington, Wyoming	Department of the Treasury Internal Revenue Service Ogden, UT 84201-0002	Internal Revenue Service P.O. Box 802501 Cincinnati, OH 45280-2501
Arizona, New Mexico	Department of the Treasury Internal Revenue Service Austin, TX 73301-0002	Internal Revenue Service P.O. Box 802501 Cincinnati, OH 45280-2501
Arkansas, Connecticut, Delaware, District of Columbia, Illinois, Indiana, Iowa, Kentucky, Maine, Maryland, Massachusetts, Minnesota, Missouri, New Hampshire, New Jersey, New York, Oklahoma, Rhode Island, Vermont, Virginia, West Virginia, Wisconsin	Department of the Treasury Internal Revenue Service Kansas City, MO 64999-0002	Internal Revenue Service P.O. Box 931000 Louisville, KY 40293-1000
Florida, Louisiana, Mississippi, Texas	Department of the Treasury Internal Revenue Service Austin, TX 73301-0002	Internal Revenue Service P.O. Box 1214 Charlotte, NC 28201-1214
Pennsylvania	Department of the Treasury Internal Revenue Service Kansas City, MO 64999-0002	Internal Revenue Service P.O. Box 802501 Cincinnati, OH 45280-2501
A foreign country, U.S. possession or territory*, or use an APO or FPO address, or file Form 2555 or 4563, or are a dual-status alien	Department of the Treasury Internal Revenue Service Austin, TX 73301-0215	Internal Revenue Service P.O. Box 1303 Charlotte, NC 28201-1303

*If you live in American Samoa, Puerto Rico, Guam, the U.S. Virgin Islands, or the Northern Mariana Islands, see Pub. 570.

Figure 4. Where to Mail Your 1040 (tax year 2021)

What Do You Need?

Before you start preparing your taxes, you need to gather **all your tax documents**, starting with W-2s, 1099s, and other records. In order to receive credits and deductions, related expenses and receipts are necessary.

In addition, for anybody on the tax return, you will need **personal information**, such as Social Security Numbers (SSNs), the correct spelling of everyone's name, and date of birth. Although basic, this information is critical. If any of the personal data is inaccurate, the IRS will reject the tax return, delaying processing and refunds.

Taxes can be stressful, but they are unavoidable. You can make the process less taxing by proactively organizing your documents into an **annual folder, binder, or an envelope**. Indicate the tax year on it, such as **Tax Year 20XX**. Throughout the year, put anything for that tax year *(e.g., receipts, documents, statements, notes, etc.)* in that annual tax folder, including a copy of final tax return.

Below is a list of items that you may need before you start preparing your taxes. You can get a pdf version of this checklist at www.understand1040.com/resources.

PERSONAL INFO

- ☐ Names, birth dates, SS and/or TIN numbers
- ☐ IRS security Identity Protection PIN (IP PIN)
- ☐ Bank account and routing number
- ☐ Copy of last year's tax return
- ☐ Prior year's AGI *(Adjusted Gross Income)*
- ☐ Any IRS tax letters received during the year
- ☐ Any out of state work or property information
- ☐ Foreign bank account info with peak value amount during the year

DEPENDENTS

- ☐ *If applicable,* Form 8332 releasing the child's custodial parent right to claim a child to the noncustodial parent
- ☐ Income of dependents and of other adults in your home

PAYMENTS

- ☐ Estimated tax payments made for federal and state, including amounts and dates
- ☐ Amount of last year's return over-payment applied to current year

INCOME

EMPLOYED

- ☐ Wages, salaries, tips and bonuses *(Form W-2)*
- ☐ Scholarship above education expenses
- ☐ Foreign earned income

UNEMPLOYED

- ☐ Unemployment compensation *(Form 1099-G)*

SELF-EMPLOYMENT

- ☐ Non-employee compensation for self-employed *(Form 1099-NEC)*
- ☐ Third-party transactions or drive-share payments such as Uber, Lyft *(Form 1099-K)*
- ☐ Cash income

SAVINGS & INVESTMENTS

- ☐ Interest income *(Form 1099-INT)*
- ☐ Dividends income *(Form 1099-DIV)*
- ☐ Sale of stock, land, etc. for capital gains, dates of acquisition, and records of your costs in property you sold *(if basis not reported on Form 1099-B)*
- ☐ Installment sale information *(Form 6252)*

RETIREMENT INCOME

- ☐ Retirement income from pensions, annuities, and IRAs *(Form 1099-R)*
- ☐ Social Security and railroad retirement *(Form SSA-1099)*

OTHER INCOME

- ☐ Miscellaneous income such as rent, prizes, and awards, royalty or other *(Form 1099-MISC)*
- ☐ Last year's state refund *(Form 1099-G)*
- ☐ Income from partnerships, trusts, and S-Corporations *(Form K-1)*
- ☐ Gambling winnings, lottery and loss records *(Form W-2G)*
- ☐ Sale of real estate property or home *(Form 1099-S)*
- ☐ Jury duty pay
- ☐ Hobby income *(expenses are no longer deductible)*
- ☐ Cancellation of credit card or other debt *(Form 1099-C)*
- ☐ Virtual currency trade information

- ☐ Record of alimony paid/received with ex-spouse's name and SSN for divorces finalized before or on December 31, 2018
- ☐ Trust income *(Schedule E)*

DEDUCTIONS

- ☐ Student loan interest *(Form 1098-E)*
- ☐ Retirement contributions *(Form 5498)*
- ☐ Health Savings Account (HSA) contributions *(Form8889)*
- ☐ Educator expenses for classroom supplies up to $250
- ☐ Sale of home info, purchase and sale date and amounts, improvements *(Form 1099-S)*
- ☐ Moving expenses for active military *(Form 3903)*
- ☐ Scholarship or fellowship records
- ☐ Nonbusiness bad debt in year it became worthless *(Form 8479 on Schedule D)*
- ☐ Standard or itemized deduction *(Schedule A)*

ITEMIZED

MEDICAL

- ☐ Medical expenses for you, your spouse & your dependents
- ☐ Health insurance premium payments
- ☐ Out of pocket doctor, dentist, hospital expenses not covered by insurance
- ☐ Prescriptions and medicines
- ☐ Travel expenses for medical purposes
- ☐ Health Savings Account (HSA) or long-term care reimbursements *(Form 1099-SA or 1099-LTC)*

TAXES

- ☐ State and local income taxes or general sales taxes
- ☐ Real estate taxes and property PIN number

- ☐ Personal property taxes
- ☐ Vehicle sales tax paid

HOME

- ☐ Mortgage interest & points paid on the first and second home, with limitations *(Form 1098)*
- ☐ Mortgage insurance premiums

CHARITABLE DONATIONS

- ☐ Cash donations *(up to $300* ***per return*** *for 2020; $300* ***per filer*** *in 2021, without itemizing)*
- ☐ Fair market value of non-cash contributions; support for donations over $250; and *(Form 8283)* for non-cash contributions over $500
- ☐ Miles driven for charitable purposes
- ☐ Unreimbursed expenses related to volunteer work

OTHER

- ☐ Gambling loses up to winning *(only if itemizing)*
- ☐ FEMA assistance info, if your county has been declared a federal disaster area
- ☐ Interest on property held for investment

CREDIT

- ☐ Child care costs—provider or person's name, address, tax id, and amount paid *(Form 2441)*
- ☐ Stimulus Payment confirmations *(otherwise called Economic Impact Payments or EIP)* or IRS Notices 1444
- ☐ Health care insurance through Marketplace for Premium Tax Credit *(Form 1095-A)*
- ☐ Adoption costs: SSN of the child; records of legal, medical and transportation costs
- ☐ Foreign taxes paid

- ☐ Receipts for any qualifying energy-efficient home improvements *(solar, windows, etc.)*
- ☐ Education tuition & other qualified education expenses *(Form 1098-T)*

BUSINESS - SCHEDULE C

- ☐ Tax or EIN number for your business
- ☐ Business income

BUSINESS EXPENSES

- ☐ Records of all business expenses, including home office, *if applicable*
- ☐ Business-use of asset information *(cost, date placed inservice, etc.)* for depreciation
- ☐ Use of vehicle and tax deductible miles
- ☐ Self-employed health insurance premium payments
- ☐ Keogh, SEP, SIMPLE and other self-employed pension plans contributions

RENTAL - SCHEDULE E

- ☐ Rental income and expenses
- ☐ Rental asset information *(cost, date placed inservice, etc.)* for depreciation
- ☐ Number of days used for personal vs. rental

FARM - SCHEDULE F

- ☐ Farm income and expenses
- ☐ Farm asset information *(cost, date placed inservice, etc.)* for depreciation

Who Should File Form 1040

As shown in **Table 5**, most taxpayers have to file Form 1040 if they work and have a gross income above a certain amount. That is called the **filing requirement**. It is based on three factors: **gross income, filing status, and age**.

Table 5. Income Filing Requirement for 2021

Filing Status	Age at the end of 2021	Gross income over
Single (S)	under 65	$12,550
	> 65	+ $1,700
MFJ	under 65 *(both spouses)*	$25,100
	> 65	+ $1,350 per spouse
MFS	any age	$5
HOH	under 65	$18,800
	> 65	+ $1,700
QW	under 65	$25,100
	> 65	+ $1,350

Draft 1040 Instructions for 2021:
***Chart A**: https://www.irs.gov/pub/irs-dft/i1040gi--dft.pdf*

However, there are additional reasons why a taxpayer may need to file a tax return, even if their income is below the threshold amount.[59] **For example**, if you are self-employed and your net earnings are above $400, you must file a tax return. Similarly, taxpayers who receive subsidies toward their marketplace health coverage also have to file taxes each year.

[59] *Chart A, B, and C: https://www.irs.gov/pub/irs-dft/i1040gi--dft.pdf*

Below is a list of reasons why you **may need to file taxes** even if your gross income is below the filing requirement threshold:

- You have a **net self-employment income of $400** or more.
- You owe ATM tax.
- You had an **additional tax on a retirement** plan such as IRA.[60]
- You owe SS and Medicare tax for household employees and need to file Schedule H.[61]
- You owe SS and Medicare tax on tips you didn't report to your employer.
- You have **received HSA** or Archer MSA **distributions**.
- You had wages over $108.28 from church or another qualified organization.
- You have received **advanced premium tax credit (APTC) payments** for health care coverage through the Marketplace. Include Form 1095-A with your filing.
- You earned foreign wages or paid foreign taxes.

Additionally, even if you don't have to file for any of the reasons listed above, you should so that you can get a refund of any federal income tax withheld or to receive refundable credits.

The main reasons to **file even if you don't have to**:

- You had federal or state i**ncome tax withheld**.
- You made estimated tax payments.

[60] *You can also just file Form 5329 by itself, if that is the only reason you are filing taxes.*
[61] *You can also just file Schedule H by itself, if that is the only reason you are filing.*

- You experienced losses on the sale of your investments that can be carried forward against future income.
- **You qualify for refundable credits** such as Earned Income Tax Credit (EITC), Premium Tax Credit (PTC), Child Tax Credit (CTC), Recovery Rebate Credit (RRC), part of American Opportunity Credit (AOTC), Child and Dependent Care Expenses (CDCE), and others. You can receive these credits as refunds even if your tax liability is zero and you have no filing requirement.
- You want to **start the statute of the limitation** period for an IRS examination. If you never file your tax return, the IRS has no time limit to review it.[62]
- To **prevent identity theft** by someone else using your personal information.
- You are a debtor in Chapter 7 or Chapter 13 bankruptcy case.[63]

Finally, **taxpayers who are dependents** have different filing requirements, which are a bit complicated. Specifically, the filing requirement for dependents is tested based on their **age, blindness, earned, unearned and gross income**. See **Table 6** for the filing requirements for a single dependent. Refer to IRS Publication 501 for filing requirements for married dependents.

---

[62] *https://www.americanbar.org/groups/business_law/publications/blt/2017/08/06_wood/*
[63] *https://irssolution.com/blog/chapter-11-bankruptcy/*

Table 6. Filing Requirement for a Single Dependent

	Unearned Income (UI)	Earned Income (EI)	Gross Income
	> $1,100	$12,550	>$1,100 or EI >**$12,550** *($12,200 + $350)*
>65 or blind	> $2,800	$14,250	>$2,800 or EI >**$14,250** *($12,200 + $2,050)*
>65 **and** blind	> $4,500	$15,950	>$4,500 or EI >**$15,950** *($12,200 + $3,750)*

**Table 2: https://www.irs.gov/pub/irs-pdf/p501.pdf*

Ways to File

The best way to file your income tax returns is by e-filing. **90% of taxpayers file electronically.**[64] E-filing is quick, safe, reliable, and a preferred method of the IRS.[65]

E-filed returns have 20% fewer clerical and math errors. The best way to **avoid math errors** is to use tax preparation software. **Tax software does most calculations and flags common errors.** It will prompt you when something is missing and often won't let you e-file until everything is fixed.

If you end up e-filing with incorrect personal information, the IRS will reject the return and give you an option to fix it before you re-file. On the other hand, if you send your tax returns with mistakes via paper, you won't know that you made errors for weeks.

Direct Deposit

The fastest way to receive a refund is by selecting direct deposit, as 8 out of 10 taxpayers choose to do so. **9 out of 10 refunds issued by the IRS take less than 21 days.**[66] Selecting to e-file and opting for a direct deposit reduces the number of weeks the tax return is processed, and the money hits the bank, from an average of 8 weeks to 1-3 weeks. If you provide incorrect bank information for direct deposit, the IRS will send you a check instead.

---

[64] *https://www.irs.gov/pub/irs-utl/oc-e-file.pdf*
[65] *https://smartasset.com/taxes/irs-tax-refund-schedule*
[66] *https://www.thebalance.com/tax-refund-options-2385793*

Table 7. Refund Timing

If you (file + refund type)	Expect Refund
e-file + direct deposit	1-3 weeks
paper file + direct deposit	3 weeks
e-file + check	4 weeks
paper file + check	8 weeks

After you decide whether you want to file electronically, you need to decide how you will file your taxes. **Do you plan to use free filing options, go to a paid tax preparer, or file it yourself?**

IRS Free File

From the 153.7 million tax returns filed for the tax year 2019, 38% self-prepared their taxes using online software, while 52% went to a tax preparer (see **Figure 5**).[67] According to the IRS, **around 70% of taxpayers qualify to file using the IRS Free File** program, but only about 2% use it each year.[68]

There are two ways to utilize the free filing options:

- If your AGI is less than $72,000 *(including MFJ filers' combined income)*, then you can use the **IRS-approved Free File (IRS FF)** tax software offered by tax preparation companies or
- If your AGI is more than $72,000 and you can perform most of the calculations yourself, you can use the **Free File Fillable Forms**.

[67] *https://www.efile.com/efile-tax-return-direct-deposit-statistics/*

[68] *https://www.irs.gov/pub/irs-utl/How%20to%20Free%20File%20Infographic_508%20FINAL.pdf*

Most IRS FF tax software only covers federal filing, but some also offer free state tax returns. Unfortunately, some of them also have additional criteria based on age or location, which adds to taxpayer confusion.

The Free File Fillable forms are electronic pdfs that can be filled out and transmitted online. However, they have limited error checking and perform basic calculations only.

Somebody with a simple tax situation can definitely take advantage of these options. However, a more complicated taxpayer may want to consider the alternatives listed below.

Free Tax Return Preparation Sites

For over 50 years, the IRS has been working with third-party partners to provide free in-person options for taxpayers.

The taxpayers can take advantage of these options by visiting a free in-person site run by:

- The IRS **Volunteer Income Tax Assistance (VITA)**
- The IRS **Tax Consulting for the Elderly (TCE)** or
- The **AARP Foundation's Tax-Aide** program.[69]

To find your closest location, visit the IRS website.[70]

The **in-person free filing options are very generous** and vary based on the program running them. The IRS manages all, and the volunteers who staff them must be IRS-certified by passing tax law training each year.

---

[69] *Technically AARP program runs the TCE sites, but they are very large and have a good options on their website of finding locations where you can get tax help.*
[70] *https://www.irs.gov/individuals/free-tax-return-preparation-for-qualifying-taxpayers*

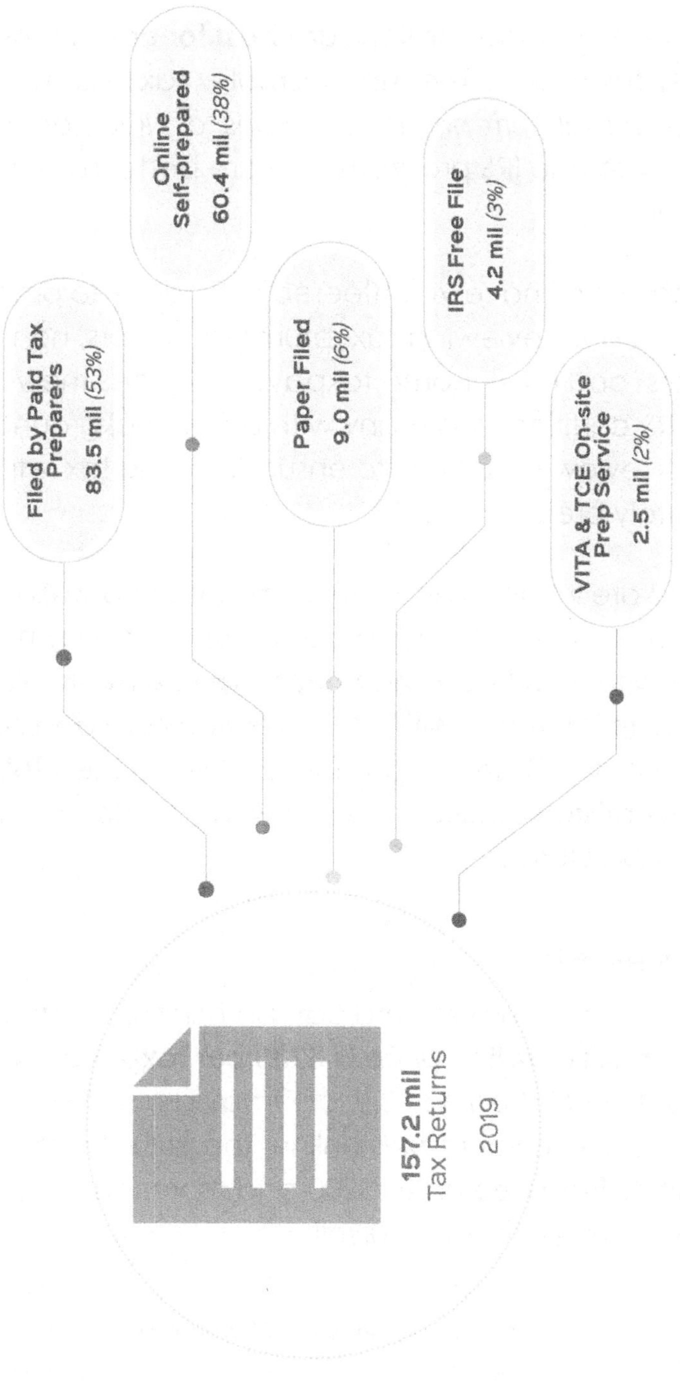

Figure 5. How U.S. Taxpayers Filed Their 2019 Taxes

The free in-person options **are best for easy to medium difficulty tax returns**. The most complex tax returns *(e.g., rental income, virtual currency transactions, or NOLs)* are out of scope under the IRS program and are better suited for paid preparers.

Since 2017, I have volunteered with all three programs preparing and reviewing tax returns for seniors, non-English speakers, and low-income taxpayers. Besides the volunteers being IRS-certified and many with a tax background, there are also review processes to ensure that the tax returns are accurately prepared.

If you are in the military, your tax return consists of several unique rules, which even paid tax preparers may not be familiar with. **Two free-filing options specialize in military filings.** One is through **MilTax**,[71] a service provided by the Department of Defense; another is through the **VITA program on many military bases**,[72] staffed with volunteers certified in military tax returns.

Paid Options

Filing taxes with a tax pro can be expensive - the **average tax return preparation price is $230 per taxpayer**, while business filers *(Schedule C, E, or F)* pay around $440.[73] Even if you self-prepare your taxes online, the price for tax software can range from free up to $200 and more, and you have to do the tax preparation yourself.

---

[71] *https://www.militaryonesource.mil/financial-legal/tax-resource-center/miltax-military-tax-services/*

[72] *https://www.military.com/discounts/free-tax-preparation-for-military.html*

[73] *pg 109: https://www.irs.gov/pub/irs-pdf/i1040gi.pdf*

Many tax software companies advertise free filing options on their websites. However, they are not the same as the IRS FF on the agency's website. Sometimes, **taxpayers who start with a free version** on the tax preparation companies' websites **end with a paid one**. Just by adding a form to your tax return, it can upgrade you to a paid version.

ProPublica has reported extensively on the dark patterns tactics.[74] Some companies offer "free" options that end up costing taxpayers by not being transparent.[75]

If you decide to hire a tax preparer to help you with your taxes, you must remember that **you are still responsible for any mistakes on your tax returns**. That is why it is imperative to pick a tax preparer that you can trust, especially if your tax return is complex. The IRS has a **database of federal tax preparer credentials and qualifications**.[76]

A great additional benefit of using the IRS FF and free in-person VITA options is not being bombarded by **extra offers and products**. For example, when you select paid tax preparation software or go to a paid tax preparer, you are often urged to purchase extra products,[77] such as:

- **Refund advanced loans** - loans against your incoming refund for faster access to the money;
- **Refund transfers** - using your refund to pay for tax services (around $34-$40).

[74] *https://www.propublica.org/article/inside-turbotax-20-year-fight-to-stop-americans-from-filing-their-taxes-for-free*
[75] *https://www.propublica.org/article/turbotax-just-tricked-you-into-paying-to-file-your-taxes*
[76] *If you are curious, you can even check my credentials, just check for my full name Agnieszka Stepinska https://irs.treasury.gov/rpo/rpo.jsf*
[77] *https://www.propublica.org/article/where-is-my-tax-refund-1?*

- **Audit support services** - extra protection in cases your tax return gets audited.
- **Tax identity protection** - extra coverage to help you resolve any tax identity fraud.

These additional products can cost $0, $20, $40, or even over $70. Some, like advanced loans, are 'free' in the sense that you don't pay for them upfront, but they are incorporated into the overall tax preparation fee, or they serve as a marketing tool.

Figure 6 below reveals the advantages and disadvantages of each filing choice.

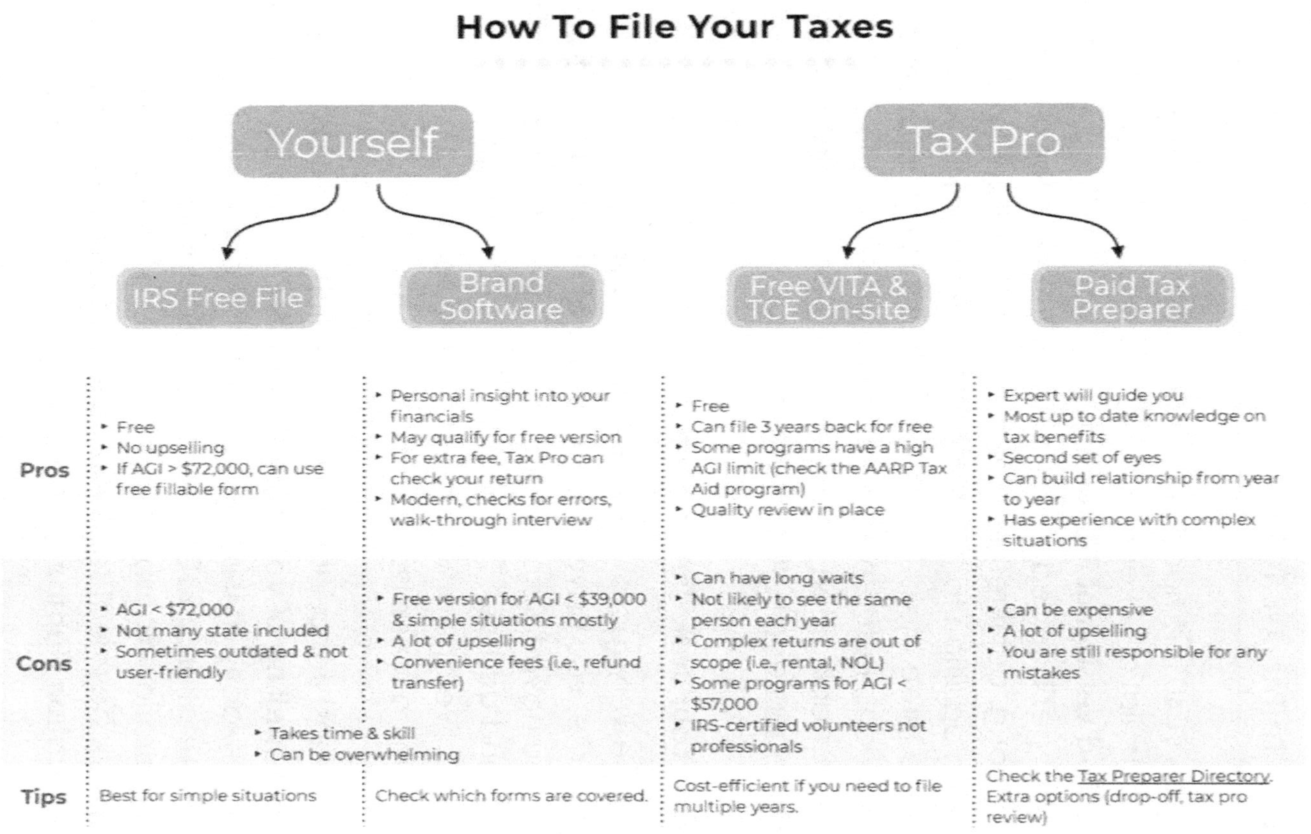

Figure 6. Filing Options

How To Prepare 1040

Form 1040 is divided into sections and contains step-by-step calculations. Keep in mind that we are going through **a simplified version of the form** to help you see the big picture and not get bogged down in the details. The form is two pages long, but it references many other schedules and forms. In addition to the two pages of Form 1040, we will go over the three main schedules that flow into our tax return calculations. Reference a version of 1040 from the IRS website, back of the Appendix, or get an annotated copy at www.understand1040.com/resources.

Fill In Your Basic Information

At the very top of Form 1040, before you even provide your name, you have to **choose one of the five filing statuses**. Then you have to provide your **name, Social Security number (SSN)**, and **address**. The address should be where you currently live and where the IRS should send all communications and refunds.

The most important information on the tax return is the **correct spelling of your name and SSN**. Your name should be spelled exactly as it is written on your SS card. The IRS matches the information on 1040 against the Social Security Administration database, and if it doesn't match, the tax return will be rejected. If you have an **Individual Taxpayer Identification Number (ITIN)**, put that on the SSN line.

For married taxpayers, all the data for your spouse has to be listed as well. **For dependents** on the return, you have to note your relationship and provide their information. Additionally, the boxes for the **Child Tax Credit (CTC)** or **Credit for Other Dependents (COD)** need to be checked. If you use tax software or work with a tax preparer, they will do that for you. If you are paper filing, you have to verify that your dependents qualify you for either of the credits before you check them. Otherwise, the credits could be disallowed, and you could receive an IRS examination letter.

Step 1 - 6. Refund or Amount Due Calculations

To calculate the amount of your refund or how much you owe in taxes, Form 1040 breaks up the tax computations into six steps (*see **Table 8** below*). **Table 9** presents an easy example we will use throughout the book to go through each step and calculation. You can download some of the tables at www.understand1040.com/resources for free or all for a minimal fee.

Table 8. Simplified 1040 Tax Calculations

step 1		**Total Income** *(L9)*
	+	Additions to Income
	-	Subtractions from Income
step 2	=	**AGI** *(L11)*
		AGI
	-	Standard or Itemized Deduction
	-	QBI
step 3	=	**Taxable Income** *(L15)*
		Taxable Income
	*	Tax Rate
step 4	=	**Tax** *(L16)*
		Tax
	+	Other Taxes
	-	Non-refundable Credits
step 5	=	**Total Tax** *(24)*
		Total Tax
	-	Payments
	-	Refundable Credits
step 6	=	**Refund** *(L34)* **or Amount Due** *(L37)*

Step 1. Report Your Total Income

Your **Total Income *(L9)***, often referred to as gross income, includes earned and unearned types of pay. **Earned income** comes mainly from labor received as wages, salary, self-employment, tips, commissions, and bonuses. **Unearned income** is from passive activities such as investments, rentals, or retirement and is reported as dividends, interest, capital gains, Social Security (SS), pensions, or annuity.

The best income is income that is not taxable, such as life insurance proceeds, municipal bond interest, disability income, child support, etc. If you make under certain gross amount, none of the income is taxable *(see **Table 5**)*. The Taxable and Non-Taxable Table in the Appendix divides different types of income between that which is taxable and which is not.

All additional taxable income not directly listed on 1040 is listed on Schedule 1, Part I *(**Table 10**)* and added to Total Income *(L9)*.

In our example, our single taxpayer had $66,900 of Total Income from variety of sources, including $3,500 from additional income listed on Sch 1, Part I.

Table 9. 1040 Tax Return Example for Single Filer (2021)

Item *(line on 1040)*	**Add**	**Subtract**	**Total**
Wages, salaries *(1)*	$60,000		
Taxable interest, dividends. Sch B *(2b,3b)*	$400		
Taxable IRA, pension, annuity & taxable social security *(4b,5b,6b)*	$2,500		
Capital gain or (loss). Sch D *(7)*	$500		
Other income - Sch 1, Part I & Sch C, E, F *(8)*	$3,500		
Total Income *(9)*			**$66,900**
Adjustments to income - Sch 1, Part II *(10)*		$4,250	
Adjusted Gross Income (AGI) *(11)*			**$62,650**
Standard or itemized (Sch A) deduction & charitable deduction & QBI *(12-13)*		$12,550	
Taxable income *(15)*			$50,100
Tax (from tax table) *(16)*			**$6,776**
Other tax - Sch 2, Part I *(17)*	$250		
Non-refundable child tax credit or credit for other dependents *(19)*		$500	
Non-refundable credits - Sch 3, Part I *(20)*		$1,750	
Other tax - Sch 2, Part II including self-employment tax *(23)*	$350		
Total Tax *(24)*			**$5,126**
Federal withholdings, estimate & prior year prepayments *(25-26)*		$4,500	
Refundable credits such as EITC, CTC & ACTC, AOTC, RRC *(27-30)*		$500	
Refundable credits - Sch 3, Part II *(31)*		$800	
Total Payments *(33)*		**$5,800**	
Refund *(34)*			**$674**
Amount you owe *(37)*			-

IRS Form 1040
**You can also calculate tax amount online by using tax calculator at: https://www.taxslayer.com/tax-tools/tax-refund-calculator*

Step 2. Calculate Your AGI

After you arrive at your total income, you can **subtract deductions listed on Sch 1, Part II** *(Table 10)*, including educator expenses, HSA deduction, half of the self-employment tax, student loan interest deduction, and traditional IRA deduction. Once you subtract these items from your total income, you arrive at **Adjusted Gross Income (AGI)** ***(L11)***.

AGI is an important item on your tax return. It is frequently referenced in determining qualifications for credits. Plus, prior year AGI is regularly used for verification purposes by tax preparation software.

In our example, our taxpayer had $4,250 worth of deductions. The deductions were subtracted from her Total Income of $66,900 to arrive at $62,650 AGI. Deductions are valuable benefits because they reduce the amount of income subject to tax (taxable income).

Table 10. Sch 1 (1040) Additional Income & Adjustments

Part I: Additional Income		
1	Taxable refunds	$250
2a	Alimony received	
2b	Divorce date (must be before 12/31/2018)	
3	Business income	$2,000
4	Other income	
5	Rental / royalties / partnerships	$250
6	Farm income	
7	Unemployment	$1,000
9	Other income	
10	**Total** *(Form 1040 line 8)*	**$3,500**
Part II: Adjustments to Income (Deductions)		
11	Educator expenses	$250
12	Business expenses	
13	HSA deduction	$1,000
14	Military moving expenses	
15	Self-employment tax	
16	Self-employment retirement plan	
17	Self-employment health insurance	
18	Savings withdrawal penalty	
19	Alimony paid	
20	IRA deduction	$2,500
21	Student loan interest	$500
23	Archer MSA deduction	
25	Other adjustments	
26	**Total** *(Form 1040 line 10a)*	**$4,250**

IRS Schedule 1 (Form 1040)

Step 3. Claim Your Deductions

After arriving at AGI, you can subtract one of the most significant deductions on your tax return —either **the standard deduction or itemized deduction *(Sch A)***. The standard deduction amount varies based on your filing status, age, and whether or not you are blind *(**Table 11**)*.

Table 11. Standard Deduction for Tax Year 2021

	Single	HOH	MFJ	MFS	QW
	$12,550	$18,800	$25,100	$12,550	$25,100
Extra for each —> if over > 65 or blindness					
	$1,700	$1,700	$1,350	$1,350	$1,350

Before the passing of the TCJA in 2018, about 31% of taxpayers itemized. However, because of the increase in the standard deduction to almost double that from the tax year 2017 and reduced value of certain itemized deductions, **in the tax year 2018, only 14% of taxpayers itemized.**[78]

The advantage of the standard deduction is that you don't have to provide any supporting documentation to receive it. However, taxpayers always have an option of itemizing[79] if it is better for them. If you choose to itemize, you have to substantiate your deductions with records supporting mortgage interest, real estate taxes, health care, and other expenses.

---

[78] *https://taxfoundation.org/standard-deduction-itemized-deductions-current-law-2019/*

[79] *Except taxpayer filing MFS whose spouse itemizes or a taxpayer for a period that is less than 12 months. https://www.irs.gov/taxtopics/tc501*

After deducting the standard or itemized deduction from AGI, you can subtract two other deductions that don't require itemization. First, introduced in the tax year 2020 and only available for taxpayers who use the standard deduction, **taxpayers can deduct up to $300 per filer for a charitable donation.**[80]

The second valuable deduction for taxpayers who are self-employed, have a business or a rental, is the **Qualified Business Income (QBI) deduction**. QBI is very advantageous and can be up to 20% of your taxable or QBI income, so always check if you qualify to claim it.

After subtracting the standard, itemized, charity, and QBI deduction, you arrive at **Taxable Income *(L15)***.

In our example, our single taxpayer opted for the standard deduction of $12,550 for the tax year 2021. That amount was subtracted from AGI to arrive at a taxable income of $50,100.

Step 4. Calculate Your Tax

To figure out the amount of tax due for the tax year, we need to **use the tax brackets and rates for your filing status**. Because our **federal tax system is progressive**, higher-income gets taxed at higher rates than lower-income, incrementally. There are two ways to figure out how much tax you are liable for the year.

---

[80] *There was a slight change in the amount of charitable donation being deductible in the tax year 2020 vs. 2021. For 2020, taxpayers could deduct up to $300 per tax return, while in 2021, taxpayers can deduct up to $300 per filer (so MFJ can deduct $600 now). https://www.cnbc.com/2021/08/30/some-donors-may-get-a-smaller-tax-benefit-for-2021-charitable-gifts.html*

The first way is to calculate the tax by using the tax brackets and rates for your filing status (***Table 12***). Tax brackets for all other filing status are listed in the Appendix. *For example*, for the tax year 2021, all taxable income up to $9,950 for a single filer gets taxed at 10%. If the single filer makes more than that, the income between $9,951 and $40,525 ($40,525 - $9,951 = $30,574) gets taxed at the next tax rate of 12%.

As in our single filer example, since the taxpayer earns even more ($50,100), the next bracket of income (from $40,526 to $50,100 => $9,574) gets taxed 22%. So the total tax liability for our filer would be computed as:

($9,950 * 10%)+ ($30,574 * 12%) + ($9,574 * 22%) =>

$995 + $3,669 + $2,106 = **$6,770**

Table 12. Income Tax Brackets for Single (2021)

Rate	Single (S)	Tax Amount *(L16)*
10%	$0 to $9,950	10% of taxable income
12%	$9,951 to $40,525	$995 + 12% over $9,950
22%	$40,526 to $86,375	$4,664 + 22% over $40,525
24%	$86,376 to $164,925	$14,751 + 24% over $86,375
32%	$164,926 to $209,425	$33,603 + 32% over $164,925
35%	$209,426 to $523,600	$47,843 + 35% over $209,425
37%	$523,601 or more	$157,804 + 37% over $523,600

The second way of calculating your tax due is by **using the Tax Tables in the 1040 instructions** *(see **Figure 7**)*. You have to locate your taxable income *(L15)* on the left of the table and select your filing status across the top. Wherever they meet is the amount of tax you are liable for the year. Again, if you are using tax software, it will perform the calculation for you.

If line 15 (taxable income) is—		And you are—			
At least	But less than	Single	Married filing jointly *	Married filing separately	Head of a household
		Your tax is—			
50,000					
50,000	**50,050**	6,754	5,605	6,754	5,719
50,050	**50,100**	6,765	5,611	6,765	5,725
50,100	**50,150**	6,776	5,617	6,776	5,731
50,150	**50,200**	6,787	5,623	6,787	5,737
50,200	**50,250**	6,798	5,629	6,798	5,743
50,250	**50,300**	6,809	5,635	6,809	5,749
50,300	**50,350**	6,820	5,641	6,820	5,755
50,350	**50,400**	6,831	5,647	6,831	5,761
50,400	**50,450**	6,842	5,653	6,842	5,767
50,450	**50,500**	6,853	5,659	6,853	5,773
50,500	**50,550**	6,864	5,665	6,864	5,779
50,550	**50,600**	6,875	5,671	6,875	5,785
50,600	**50,650**	6,886	5,677	6,886	5,791
50,650	**50,700**	6,897	5,683	6,897	5,797
50,700	**50,750**	6,908	5,689	6,908	5,803
50,750	**50,800**	6,919	5,695	6,919	5,809
50,800	**50,850**	6,930	5,701	6,930	5,815
50,850	**50,900**	6,941	5,707	6,941	5,821
50,900	**50,950**	6,952	5,713	6,952	5,827
50,950	**51,000**	6,963	5,719	6,963	5,833

Figure 7. Tax Table Example

https://www.irs.gov/pub/irs-dft/i1040tt--dft.pdf

You will note that the tax amount per the IRS tax table is $6,776, while per our mathematical computation, it was $6,770. **The slight difference is because the tax tables in the 1040 instructions have a range of income every $50.** Therefore, the tax due for our single filer is the same if she makes any amount between $50,100 and $50,150.

The tax tables are simplified to be more user-friendly and reduce the number of pages in the 1040 instruction booklet.

If we went through the mathematical computation and found out how much our taxpayer would owe in tax on $50,150 of taxable income, it would be $6,781.16. And the average of $6,770.16 and $6,781.16 is precisely $6,776, what is listed in the IRS tax table.

The tax table is for taxable income ranges every $50; therefore, it represents the average tax for each range.

Even an easier option of calculating the amount of tax due is by using **tax calculators online**. The ones I can recommend are by Nerdwallet, TaxAct, and TaxSlayer.[81] One note of caution, some calculators ask for Total Income *(L9)* while others ask for Taxable Income *(L15)*, which makes a significant difference. Remember that taxable income is the amount AFTER you subtract standard or itemized deduction and make other adjustments.

---

[81] *Nerdwallet @https://www.nerdwallet.com/taxes/tax-calculator, TaxAct @https://www.taxact.com/tools/tax-calculator, TaxSlayer @https://www.taxslayer.com/tax-tools/tax-refund-calculator*

In our example, our single taxpayer with a taxable income of $50,100 has a tax liability for the year of $6,776, based on our calculations. The taxpayer is in the 22% marginal tax bracket.

Before we finalize this section, we should discuss one more important tax term—**the effective tax rate**. We learned that our single filer was in the 22% marginal tax bracket. That meant that the last dollar of her income was taxed at 22%. However, some of her income was taxed at 10% and 12%. The **effective tax rate is closer to the average tax rate that the taxpayer pays in taxes compared to taxable income**.

If we want to compare similar items, we should take the calculated Tax amount *(L16)* and divide it by Taxable Income *(L15)*. *In our example,* the effective tax rate for our taxpayer would be 13.5% ($6,776/$50,100), which is much less than the 22% marginal tax bracket.

P.S. Note: It is crucial to understand precisely which numbers are used in the effective tax rate calculation. While working on this section, I came across several resources discussing effective tax rates but using different numbers for the calculations.

For example, *The Street*, *TaxAct*, *The Balance*, *U.S. News*, and *Investopedia* have used the calculations as described above. On the other hand, *Credit Karma* was taking Total Tax *(L24)* and dividing it by Taxable Income *(L15)*, while the *College Investor* was taking Tax amount *(L16)* and dividing it by AGI *(L10)*. And then finally, some other sources were very vague about how they were performing the calculation *(Bankrate)*.

Step 5. Claim Your Non-refundable Tax Credits and Calculate Total Tax

Page 2 of Form 1040 is more complex and can feel repetitive because of the multiple additions and subtractions that need to be done and don't seem in a logical order.

The tax amount that we calculated is a starting point to figuring out what you actually owe or receive as a refund for the year. After calculating our Tax *(L16)*, we have to refer to **Sch 2 for any additional taxes**. First, we add AMT and advanced premium tax credit repayments from Part I *(L17) of Sch 2*. Then, we need to perform two subtractions before adding other taxes from Part II (***Table 13***).

Non-refundable credits, mainly the child tax credit, credit for other dependents *(L19)* and other non-refundable credits listed on Sch 3, Part I *(L20)*, are deducted. The credits listed on Sch 3 Part I include foreign tax credit, education credits, retirement savings contribution credit, adoption credit, etc. **(Table 14)**. **These subtractions are a dollar-for-dollar reduction in tax liability.**

The non-refundable credits can't get your due tax amount to be less than zero. So if the amount of non-refundable credit is more than what you owe in tax liability, they will reduce your tax liability to zero, and that's it.

Table 13. Sch 2 (1040) Additional Taxes

Part I: Tax		
1	AMT tax	
2	APTC Repayment	$250
3	**Total** *(Form 1040 line 17)*	**$250**
Part II: Other Taxes		
4	Self-employment tax	
5	SS & Medicare tax on Unreported Tips	
6	Uncollected SS & Medicare tax	
8	Additional tax on retirement plans	$350
9	Household employment tax	
10	Repayment of first-homebuyer credit	
11	Additional Medicare or Net Investment tax	
12	Net investment income tax	
13	Uncollected SS & Medicare tax on Tips	
14	Interest on Installment income	
15	Interest on deferred tax on installment sales	
16	Recapture of low-income housing credit	
17a-z	Other taxes	
19	Additional tax from Sch 8812	
20	Sec 965 net tax liability installment	
21	**Total** *(Form 1040 line 23)*	**$350**

IRS Schedule 2 (Form 1040)

At the final stage of calculating the Total Tax *(L24)* for the year, we go back to Sch 2, Part II *(L23)* and add other taxes such as half of the self-employment tax, household employment tax, net investment tax, additional IRA tax, etc. This addition increases your tax liability and **finalizes your Total Tax**.

Notice how splitting other taxes from Sch 2 into two places can significantly impact total tax. The non-refundable credits can reduce our tax to zero but not below; therefore, our tax liability increases after adding other taxes. Combining all the taxes and then subtracting non-refundable credits, for some taxpayers, would reduce the total tax as shown in **Table 14**.

Table 14. Order of Operations

Total Tax		**$2,000**	$2,000	Total Tax
Sch 2, Part I	$400	*Add*	$400	Sch 2, Part I
		$2,400		
Sch 3, Part I	$3,000	*Subtract*		
		$0		
Sch 2, Part II	$500	*Add*	$500	Sch 2, Part II
Total Tax		**$500**		
			$2,900	
		Subtract	$3,000	Sch 3, Part I
			$0	Total Tax

In our example, our taxpayer had $600 of additional taxes, which were added to her tax liability of $6,776 ($6,776 + $600 = $7,376). She also had some non-refundable and child tax credits of $2,250, which were subtracted from her tax liability, arriving at Total Tax of $5,126 ($7,376 - $2,250 = $5,126).

Step 6. Your Refund or Amount Owed

The **Total Tax** *(L24)* is the actual tax liability for the year. However, that is not what you will necessarily need to pay because we are still not finished. At this point, **any payments made toward your tax liability**, like federal withholdings, quarterly estimate payments, or prior year prepayments, will be subtracted from your Total Tax.

Additionally, we will subtract the most valuable type of credits– **the refundable credits** such as EITC, ACTC, AOTC, and EIPs *(L27-L30)*, plus refundable credits from Schedule 3, Part II *(**Table 15**)*. The refundable credits are most valuable because they can reduce your tax liability below zero and lead to a refund.

If the payments you made and all the refundable credits you qualify for are more than your tax liability for the year, you will receive a refund *(L34)*. However, if they are less than your Total Tax, you will have an amount due at tax time *(L37)*.

In our example, our taxpayer had $4,500 of withholdings and payments toward her tax during the tax year. She also qualified for $500 of refundable credits listed on 1040 directly and $800 from Sch 3, Part II. Therefore she will receive a refund of $674 (($4,500 + $500 + $800) - $5,126 = $674).

Table 15. Sch 3 (1040) Additional Credits & Payments

Part I: Non-refundable Credits		
1	Foreign tax credit	$50
2	Child & dependent care expenses*	
3	Education credits	$1,200
4	Retirement savings contributions credit	$500
5	Energy credits	
6a-z	Other non-refundable credits	
8	Total *(Form 1040 **line 20**)*	$1,750
Part II: Other Payments & Refundable Credits		
9	Premium Tax Credit	
10	Payments made with extension to file	
11	Excess SS tax withheld	
12	Fuel tax credit	
13	Other payments & refundable credits	
b	Sick and family leave credits	
g	Child & dependent care expenses*	$800
h	Sick and family leave credits	
15	Total *(Form 1040 **line 31**)*	$800

IRS Schedule 3 (Form 1040)
**Notice that the child and dependent care credits are listed in non-refundable (how it used to be) and refundable credit areas. The refundable section is new for tax year 2021 and available for taxpayers living in the US more than half a year.*

3 TO 5 YEAR COMPARISON

Sometimes it is hard to grasp how your tax situation changed over the past few years. The best way to do that is to **take the items described in steps 1 through 6 and compare them side by side** (see ***Table 16***).

You can download a copy for yourself at www.understand1040.com/resources. Once you gather copies of your prior tax returns, enter the information into the worksheet from the lines noted. Again, **this is a big-picture view of what changed for you.**

Especially if your family and financial circumstances haven't changed much, but your refund or tax amount due keeps changing, it could be a good indicator of the impact of tax law changes on your situation.

I am providing a link to the last five 1040 forms from the tax year 2017 until 2021. If you want to look at other years, type the address https://www.irs.gov/pub/irs-prior/f1040--XXXX.pdf and replace the XXXX with a year such as 1989. This information goes back to 1864. If you thought only the current 1040 is confusing, take a look at the 1920 form. (✿^‿^)

From examining the tax forms from 2017 until now, we started with 1040 containing 79 line items *(while now there are 38 lines)*. In the tax year 2018, after the passage of TCJA, the Form 1040 became much shorter, but **it started including additional schedules**. In the tax year 2018, there were six separate schedules, which have been reduced to three now. All the information from the 79 lines in 2017, didn't just disappear and the tax code was simplified. Instead, all the information has been moved to Schedule 1, 2, 3 as attachments.

Table 16. 5-Year Tax Return Comparison

	2021	2020	2019	2018	2017
Total Income					
	L9	*L9*	*L7b*	*L6*	*L22*
Additions to Income					
Subtractions from Income					
AGI					
	L11	*L11*	*L8b*	*L7*	*L37*
Standard or Itemized Deduction					
QBI					
Taxable Income					
	L15	*L15*	*L11b*	*L10*	*L43*
Tax					
	L16	*L16*	*L12a*	*L11a*	*L44*
Other Taxes					
Non-refundable Credits					
Total Tax					
	L24	*L24*	*L16*	*L15*	*L63*
Payments					
Refundable Credits					
Refund					
	L34	*L34*	*L20*	*L19*	*L75*
Amount Due					
	L37	*L37*	*L23*	*L22*	*L78*

The L numbers are the 1040 line items for each year, where each item is found.

2021 1040   2020 1040   2019 1040   2018 1040   2017 1040

12 Interesting Facts About 1040

Who says we can't have a little fun while talking about taxes? So here are 12 interesting facts about tax form 1040.

1. According to the IRS, **the average time to complete tax form 1040 is 12 hours.**[82] For non-business taxpayers, the time is 8 hours, while taxpayers who file Schedule C, E, or F spend about 21 hours in total to gather, plan and complete their tax returns.

2. **The average tax preparation cost is $230 per tax return.** That can start as low as free to $140 for simple returns, up to over $440 for Form 1040s with Schedules C, E, or F.

3. Form 1040 is not just difficult for average folks. Even Einstein once said, ***"The hardest thing in the world to understand is the income tax."*** On the two pages of Form 1040 there are 7 references to other schedules, 7 to other forms, and the taxpayer is asked 14 times to "see instructions" to the 1040.

4. According to the IRS forms database, the oldest 1040 tax form dates to 1864.[83] It was created after Abraham Lincoln levied the first income tax to help pay for the Civil War effort. The right to impose a Federal income tax was ratified on Feb 3, 1913, with the passing of the 16th Amendment. This is the time when a closer replica to 1040 was born.

---

[82] *Pg 109 of 1040 Instructions: https://www.irs.gov/pub/irs-pdf/i1040gi.pdf*
[83] *https://www.irs.gov/pub/irs-prior/f1040--1864.pdf*

5. Tax returns are protected by law from unauthorized disclosure. However, if you want to see **tax returns that have been released to the public**, look no further than the **tax returns of presidential candidates** going back to Franklin Roosevelt and ending with the current president Joe Biden.[84] Some tax returns look like average upper-middle-class Americans, such as for Bernie Sanders, while others are those of millionaires, like Hillary Clinton or Jeb Bush.[85]

6. Form 1040 is only **one of 800 other IRS income tax forms and schedules.**[86]

7. Since 1976, taxpayers have allocated over $1.5 billion to the Presidential Election Fund *(PEF)* by checking the PEF checkbox on their tax returns.[87] As of Oct 2021, the fund had over $400 million. In 1976, roughly 28% of taxpayers selected to have funds moved to PEF, while only 4% did so on the 2020 tax returns.

8. Tax form 1040 **is a legal document** which you make binding when you sign and date: "*Under penalties of perjury, I declare that I have examined this return and accompanying schedules and statements, and to the best of my knowledge and belief, they are true, correct, and complete.*"

---

[84] *https://www.taxnotes.com/presidential-tax-returns*
[85] *To address the elephant in the room, there is also a single tax return for former President Trump dating back to 2005.*
[86] *https://www.theatlantic.com/ideas/archive/2019/04/american-tax-returns-dont-need-be-painful/586369/*
[87] *https://www.fec.gov/introduction-campaign-finance/understanding-ways-support-federal-candidates/presidential-elections/public-funding-presidential-elections/*

9. You are not wrong when you think it is hard to read Form 1040. The font used on the standard 1040 is **Helvetica size 8 pt, with 10 pt for headings**. The 1040-SR for seniors has a larger font of 11 pt for body and 12 pt for headings. Since 2012, the 1040 has a mint background (hex color #dbfffa).

10. A quick and easy way to find instructions to Form 1040 or any other IRS tax form is to click on the link at the bottom of it that says: "*Go to www.irs.gov/Form1040 for instructions and the latest information.*"

11. As of 2021, there are 8 different variations of Form 1040[88]:

A. 1040 - standard form;
B. 1040-SR for seniors;
C. 1040-NR for nonresident aliens;
D. 1040-SS for residents of US territories;
E. 1040-PR is a Spanish version of 1040-SS;
F. 1040-ES is used to pay estimated quarterly taxes;
G. 1040-V is a short payment voucher to pay yearly tax, and
H. 1040-X is a form to file an amendment.

[88] *https://www.investopedia.com/taxes/seniors-get-new-simplified-tax-form/*

12. Per IRS law, you are required to report all your income, including income form "*illegal activities, such as money from dealing illegal drugs, bribes, kickbacks, etc.*"[89] It needs to be reported under "other income" on Sch 1 of 1040. It is called: "Follow the money." Considering the number of criminals found guilty and sent to jail not for the criminal activity that they engaged in but rather tax evasion:[90]

A. Al Capone in 1931;
B. Salvatore Demeo in 2018,
C. Irving Wexler in 1933
D. John Gotti in 1992.

[89] *https://taxfoundation.org/irs-guidance-thieves-drug-dealers-and-corrupt-officials/*
[90] *https://www.findlaw.com/legalblogs/criminal-defense/why-organized-crime-bosses-get-arrested-for-tax-evasion/*

TEST YOUR KNOWLEDGE

The main point of this book is to teach you about the US Form 1040 that is used to file your federal tax returns. The easiest way to check your progress is to have a little fun and test your knowledge with a quiz.

This is an additional opportunity to learn about your tax returns, so don't worry if you get stuck on a question. Instead, go to the answer section, where you can find in-depth explanations of the answers.

1. Typically, not including extensions, your tax returns are due on:

A. May 17
B. April 15
C. April 15
D. July 15
E. October 15

2. What is the tax form used most often to file individual taxes?

A. 1040-SR
B. 1040-EZ
C. 1040-A
D. 1040

3. What are the tax filing statuses?

A. Dependent
B. Head of Household
C. Single
D. Married Filing Jointly
E. Senior
F. Qualifying Widow(er)
G. Married Considered as Unmarried
H. Married Filing Separately

4. What are two significant deductions that all taxpayers can take?

A. Family deduction
B. Standard deduction
C. Business deduction
D. Itemized deduction

5. What is the effective tax bracket?

A. The value of deductions and credits for the amount of taxable income.
B. The amount of additional tax paid for every extra dollar earned as income.
C. The lowest income tax bracket.
D. The percentage of your income that you pay in taxes.

6. What is the difference between a tax deduction and a tax credit?

A. Deductions are worth half what credits are worth.
B. Deductions reduce your taxable income, while credits reduce your tax due.
C. They are the same.
D. Credits reduce your gross income, while deductions reduce your taxable income.

7. What is AGI and where is it on 1040?

A. It stands for Adjusted Gross Income, which is income after adjustments. It is found on line 11 of 1040.
B. It stands for Average Gross Income, total income calculated after subtracting standard or itemized deduction. Found on line 15 of 1040.
C. The total from paychecks you receive from your employer after taxes.
D. It stands for Accounting Group Instruction, a group that designs and publishes tax forms.

8. Where do you find how much total tax you are liable for the year?

A. Line 16 of 1040, Tax.
B. Line 24 of 1040, Total Tax.
C. Line 34 of 1040, Refunds or Line 37, Amount you owe.
D. Line 25 of 1040, Federal withholdings.

9. Where do you find how much withholding you had from Forms W-2s and 1099s?

A. It is not on Form 1040. You have to check your paychecks or W-2 Forms.
B. Line 25a on 1040.
C. Line 25 on 1040, Federal income tax withheld.
D. Line 33 on 1040, Total payments.

10. What is EITC and where do you determine whether you qualified for and received it?

A. It is Earned Income Tax Credit *(EITC)* on line 27a of 1040. EITC is a credit for taxpayers with children who receive it from their employer.
B. It is an End Income Tax Calculation for end-of-year income.
C. It is Employee Income Tax Credit, found on one of the Schedules.
D. It is Earned Income Tax Credit *(EITC)* on line 27a of 1040. EITC is a credit for earning income from labor and services *(earned income)* up to certain levels.

11. Where do you determine if any of your Social Security was taxable?

A. Social Security is never taxable.

B. Total Social Security is listed on line 6a of 1040, while the taxable amount is listed on line 6b.

C. Social Security is listed together with wages on line 1 of 1040.

D. Social Security is not found on the regular Form 1040. It can only be located on Form 1040-SR for seniors.

12. Where do you locate on Form 1040 whether you received any Child Tax Credit (CTC) or additional child tax credit (ACTC)?

A. Line 19 on 1040.

B. CTC and ACTC are listed on Schedule 3 with other tax credits.

C. Line 28 on 1040.

D. Line 19 and 28 on 1040.

13. What is the exemption amount for a dependent and where is it on 1040?

A. It is worth $4,050 per dependent.

B. Personal exemptions were eliminated from federal taxes with the passing of TCJA in 2018.

C. Line 19 on 1040.

14. If you qualified for stimulus payment(s) but didn't receive any, where would you determine whether you received the Recovery Rebate Credit (RRC)?

A. You can't claim your stimulus payments on the tax return.

B. If you didn't receive the stimulus payments, it is too late.

C. Line 30 on 1040.

D. Stimulus payments are taxable and would go on line 8 of 1040 under other income.

15. How can you designate part of your refund to be applied to next year?

A. You have to call the IRS at 1-800-829-1040 and select "refund options."

B. You can't apply your refund to next year's taxes.

C. You would have to receive your refund first and then use it to pay next year's quarterly estimated taxes.

D. You can specify on line 36 of 1040 how much of your refund you want to go towards next year's taxes.

Count the number of answers that you got correctly. If you had:

0-5 Correct: There is nowhere for you to go but up. You are in the right place to learn about your tax returns. Go through the Form 1040 example to familiarize yourself with how the tax calculations determine your refund or amount due for the year.

6-10 Correct: Given the complexity of Form 1040, you did pretty well. Work through the example presented and sections most applicable to your financial and tax situation. You can boost your tax IQ even more by examining the areas you got wrong.

11-15 Correct: Congrats on your results. You have a solid foundation of Form 1040. You understand what is on your tax return and how to determine whether you received all the deductions and credits you qualify for. Keep building your skills to take advantage of all the tax benefits for your situation.

Answers

1. **The answer is (B) April 15.** For the tax year 2021, because April 15 falls on Good Friday, the tax due date is April 18, 2022. This means that the tax due date has not been April 15, even once for the past three years. However, that is the tax due date in the IRS Section 6072(a) code.[91]

E. ~~May 17, 2021~~ was the due date for the tax year 2020, which was extended due to the Covid-19 pandemic and IRS delays.

F. April 15

G. ~~July 15, 2020~~ was the due date for the tax year 2019, which was extended due to the Covid-19 pandemic.

H. ~~October 15~~ is the due date for taxpayers who file Form 4868, a 6-month extension. The extended due date gives taxpayers extra time to file, but the payment date is still April 15.

2. **The answer is (D) 1040.** Form 1040, US Individual Income Tax Return, is used to file federal income taxes.

A. ~~1040-SR~~ was first published for the tax year 2018. It is primarily to file tax returns for seniors. It has a larger font and gives greater prominence to tax benefits for taxpayers with retirement benefits.[92]

---

[91] *https://www.irs.gov/pub/irs-drop/n-11-17.pdf*
[92] *https://www.investopedia.com/taxes/seniors-get-new-simplified-tax-form/*

B. ~~1040 EZ~~ was used for simple tax returns of filers with primarily W-2 income. The form was retired in 2018.[93]

C. ~~1040 A~~ was used for taxpayers that made less than $100,000 a year and didn't itemize their taxes. The form was retired in 2018.

D. 1040

3. **The answer is (B-HOH, C - Single, D - MFJ, F - QW, H-MFS)**. There are five types of tax filing statuses.

A. ~~Dependent~~ is someone who another person financially supports. A dependent could be single or married but could not be HOH or QW. Taxpayers who file HOH or QW need to financially support their dependents.

B. Head of Household (HOH)

C. Single

D. Married Filing Jointly (MFJ)

E. ~~Senior~~ refers to a taxpayer who is over 65 years old and qualifies for the additional standard deduction. Seniors can be single, HOH, MFJ, QW, MFS. Being a senior is not a filing status.

F. Qualifying Widow(er) (QW)

G. ~~Married Considered as Unmarried~~ is a definition used to qualify married taxpayers who want to file as HOH. They have to pay more than half of the cost of keeping up a home for a dependent and had to live apart from their spouse for at least 6 months of the tax year (July-Dec).

H. Married Filing Separately (MFS)

---

[93] *https://www.irs.gov/forms-pubs/about-form-1040-ez*

4. **The answer is (B and D).** (B) The standard deduction is a flat amount that taxpayers can deduct on their taxes based on their filing status, age, and blindness. (D) Itemized deduction can be claimed on Schedule A with detailed information of various expenses, such as health care expenses, mortgage interest, real estate taxes, etc.

A. ~~Family deduction~~ - there is no such thing

B. Standard deduction

C. ~~Business deductions~~ are only available for taxpayers who have businesses.

D. Itemized deduction

5. **The answer is (D) the percentage of your income that you pay in taxes.** It is the average rate at which all your income is taxed. It is calculated by taking your tax liability and dividing it by taxable income. If your taxable income is $50,100 and you are single, your marginal tax bracket is 22%. However, your effective tax rate is much lower. At $50,100, with no other benefits, the tax liability would be $6,776. That means that the effective tax rate is 13.5% ($6,776 / $50,100). The effective tax rate doesn't take into account state, self-employment taxes or credits.

A. ~~The value of deductions and credits for the amount of taxable income.~~ There is no such tax bracket.

B. ~~The amount of additional tax paid for every additional dollar earned as income.~~ That is a marginal tax rate, which is dependent on the amount of income a taxpayer has. Currently the US tax system has 7 tax brackets - 10%, 12%, 22%, 24%, 32%, 35%, 37%. If your taxable income is $50,100 and you are single, your marginal tax bracket is 22%.

C. ~~The lowest income tax bracket.~~ From the US federal marginal tax rates of 10%, 12%, 22%, 24%, 32%, 35%, 37%, it would be the 10%.

D. The percentage of your income that you pay in taxes.

6. **The answer is (B) Deductions reduce your taxable income while credits reduce your tax due.** For example, a $500 tax deduction would reduce your taxable income from $25,000 to $24,500. On the other hand, a $500 tax credit would reduce the amount of tax you owe from $2,800 to $2,300. Thus, a tax credit is often more valuable because it reduces your taxes dollar for dollar. Some significant tax credits include EITC and AOTC. The two largest tax deductions include standard or itemized deductions.

A. ~~Deductions are worth half what credits are worth.~~

B. Deductions reduce your taxable income, while credits reduce your tax due.

C. ~~They are the same.~~

D. ~~Credits reduce your gross income, while deductions reduce your taxable income.~~

7. **The answer is (A) Adjusted Gross Income which is income after adjustments.** AGI is frequently used to check eligibility for tax deductions and to verify taxpayer identity. Found on line 11 of 1040.

A. It stands for Adjusted Gross Income, which is income after adjustments. It is found on line 11 of 1040.

B. ~~It stands for Average Gross Income, total income calculated after subtracting standard or itemized~~

~~deduction. Found on line 15 of 1040.~~ There is no such thing. AGI less standard or itemized deduction, charitable deductions, and QBI is Taxable Income on line 15 of 1040.

C. ~~Total from paychecks you received from your employer after taxes.~~ That is net earnings from your employment. You start with your gross income on the tax return, then apply deductions and credits to calculate what is taxable.

D. ~~It stands for Accounting Group Instruction, a group that designs and publishes tax forms.~~ That is not correct. The Internal Revenue Service (IRS) publishes all the tax forms.

8. **The answer is (B) Line 24 of 1040, Total Tax.** The total tax amount is calculated based on your taxable income, plus additional tax from Sch 2 such as self-employment tax and less certain non-refundable credits. That is your total tax for the year.

A. ~~Line 16 of 1040, Tax.~~ That line is the initial tax amount calculated using the tax brackets and rates for your filing status. You have to also add other taxes from Sch 2 and subtract certain non-refundable credits to find out how much in total tax liability you owe for the year.

B. Line 24 of 1040, Total Tax.

C. ~~Line 34 of 1040, Refunds or Line 37, Amount you owe.~~ Your refund or amount due is calculated after considering all other payments you made during the year through withholdings and estimated installments.

D. ~~Line 25 of 1040, Federal withholdings.~~ That is the amount of tax you withheld from W-2s and 1099 forms during the year. If you don't withhold sufficiently during the year, you will have an amount due. If you withhold too much, you will receive a refund.

9. The answer is (C) Line 25 on 140, Federal income tax withheld. Line 25a lists withholdings from regular W-2 employment. Line 25b lists withholdings on all 1099 forms, such as 1099-NEC from self-employment or 1099-DIV from investments. Line 25c lists withholdings on W-2G for gambling winnings. Together they represent the total of withholdings for the year.

A. ~~It is not on Form 1040. You have to check your paychecks or W-2 Forms.~~

B. ~~Line 25a on 1040.~~ That is partially correct. Line 25a reports withholdings from W-2 employers. However, withholdings from other forms on lines 25b and 25c, such as 1099-R, 1099-DIV, or W-2G, need to be added.

C. Line 25 on 1040, Federal income tax withheld.

D. ~~Line 33 on 1040, Total payments.~~ Total payments include refundable credits such as EITC and AOTC.

10. The answer is (D) Earned Income Tax Credit (EITC) on line 27a of 1040. EITC is a credit for earning income from labor and services *(earned income)* up to certain levels. You wouldn't qualify for the benefit if your only income was from "unearned" sources such as investments or you had earnings above certain thresholds. If you received the credit, it would show up on line 27a.

A. ~~It is Earned Income Tax Credit (EITC) on line 27a of 1040. EITC is a credit for taxpayers with children who receive it from their employer.~~ That is partially correct. It is Earned Income Tax Credit found on line 27a of 1040.

Taxpayers who have children and those without children can qualify for it if they meet certain income thresholds. The credit is claimed on the tax return.

B. ~~It is an End Income Tax Calculation for end of year income.~~

C. ~~It is Employee Income Tax Credit, found on one of the Schedules.~~

D. It is Earned Income Tax Credit (EITC) on line 27a of 1040. EITC is a credit for earning income from labor and services *(earned income)* up to certain levels.

11. The answer is (B) total Social Security is listed on line 6a of 1040, while the taxable amount is listed on line 6b. Either 0%, 50%, or 85% of Social Security can be taxable depending on the amount of other income you receive.

A. ~~Social Security is never taxable.~~

B. Total Social Security is listed on line 6a of 1040, while the taxable amount is listed on line 6b.

C. ~~Social Security is listed together with wages on line 1 of 1040.~~

D. ~~Social Security is not found on the regular Form 1040. It can be located only on Form 1040 SR for seniors.~~ That is not correct. It is found on line 6 of 1040.

12. The answer is (D) line 19 and 28 on 1040. For the tax year 2021, the CTC was split into two parts: non-refundable, listed on line 19, and refundable, listed on line 28. The change is significant because taxpayers who qualify for the refundable part can receive it even if they don't have any tax liability.

A. ~~Line 19 on 1040.~~ That is partly correct. Only the non-refundable part of CTC is listed on line 19, while the refundable amount of CTC is listed on line 28. This is a new development for the tax year 2021.

B. ~~CTC and ACTC are listed on Schedule 3 with other tax credits.~~

C. ~~Line 28 on 1040.~~ That is partly correct. That is only the refundable part of CTC. The non-refundable amount is listed on line 19.

D. Line 19 and 28 on 1040.

13. The answer is (B) personal exemptions were eliminated from federal taxes with the passing of TCJA in 2018. However, rather than being actually removed, the personal exemptions have been set to $0 *(they still stayed in the code)*. Many states still have personal expeditions on state tax returns. However, including dependents on your tax return can increase your standard deduction and qualify you for several deductions and credits.[94]

A. ~~It is worth $4,050 per dependent.~~ That is not correct. With the passing of TCJA in 2018, exemption amounts for dependents have been set to $0.

[94] *https://www.taxpolicycenter.org/taxvox/tcja-eliminated-personal-exemptions-why-are-states-still-using-them*

B. Personal exemptions were eliminated from federal taxes with the passing of TCJA in 2018.

C. ~~Line 19 on 1040.~~ That is Child Tax Credit *(CTC)* or credit for other dependents. For tax year 2021, the CTC is worth $3,600 for children under 6 and $3,000 for children between 6 and 17. The credit for other dependents is worth $500.[95]

14. The answer is (C) line 30 on 1040. In case you qualified for but didn't receive the three stimulus payments from the government. The way to claim them is to file taxes and claim the RRC on line 30 of 1040. You can claim the third stimulus payment on the tax return for 2021. The first two economic payments must be claimed on the 2020 tax returns.[96]

A. ~~You can't claim your stimulus payments on the tax return.~~

B. ~~If you didn't receive the stimulus payments, it is too late.~~ If you qualify for any economic payments, you can claim them by filing tax returns and claiming RRC.

C. Line 30 on 1040.

D. ~~Stimulus payments are taxable and would go on line 8 of 1040 under other income.~~ Stimulus payments are not taxable but must be listed on the tax returns to determine whether you received the proper amount. If the government owed you more than what you got, it would be as RRC on line 30.

---

95 *https://www.investopedia.com/ask/answers/102015/how-much-does-dependent-reduce-your-taxes.asp*

96 *https://www.irs.gov/newsroom/recovery-rebate-credit*

15. The answer is (D) you can specify on line 36 of 1040 how much of your refund you want to go towards next year's taxes.

A. ~~You have to call the IRS at 1-800-829-1040 and select "refund options."~~ You can designate on your Form 1040 line 36 to have part of your refund pre-pay next year's taxes.

B. ~~You can't apply your refund to next year's taxes.~~

C. ~~You would have to receive your refund first and then use it to pay next year's quarterly estimated taxes.~~ That is partly correct. You can always choose to go this way, but a more convenient option is to specify on line 36 of 1040 to have part of the refund go to next year.

D. You can specify on line 36 of 1040 how much of your refund you want to go towards next year's taxes.

APPENDIX

The main point of this book is to teach you about the US Form 1040 used to file your federal tax returns. The easiest way to check if this book succeeded is by letting you have a little bit of fun with a quick quiz.

TAX BRACKETS FOR 2021

Single (S)

Rate	Income Bracket	Tax owed
10%	$0 to $9,950	10% of taxable income
12%	$9,951 to $40,525	$995 + (12% over $9,950)
22%	$40,526 to $86,375	$4,664 + (22% over $40,525)
24%	$86,376 to $164,925	$14,751 + (24% over $86,375)
32%	$164,926 to $209,425	$33,603 + (32% over $164,925)
35%	$209,426 to $523,600	$47,843 + (35% over $209,425)
37%	$523,601 or more	$157,804.25 + (37% over $523,600)

Married Filing Jointly (MFJ) or Qualifying Widow(er)

Rate	Income Bracket	Tax owed
10%	$0 to $19,900	10% of taxable income
12%	$19,901 to $81,050	$1,990 + (12% over $19,900)
22%	$81,051 to $172,750	$9,328 + (22% over $81,050)
24%	$172,751 to $329,850	$29,502 + (24% over $172,750)
32%	$329,851 to $418,850	$67,206 + (32% over $329,850)
35%	$418,851 to $628,300	$95,686 + (35% over $418,850)
37%	$628,301 or more	$168,993.50 + (37% over $628,300)

Head of Household (HOH)

Rate	Income Bracket	Tax owed
10%	$0 to $14,200	10% of taxable income
12%	$14,201 to $54,200	$1,420 + (12% over $14,200)
22%	$54,201 to $86,350	$6,220 + (22% over $54,200)
24%	$86,351 to $164,900	$13,293 + (24% over $86,350)
32%	$164,901 to $209,400	$32,145 + (32% over $164,900)
35%	$209,401 to $523,600	$46,385 + (35% over $209,400)
37%	$523,601 or more	$156,355 + (37% over $523,600)

Married Filing Separately (MFS)

Rate	Income Bracket	Tax owed
10%	$0 to $9,950	10% of taxable income
12%	$9,951 to $40,525	$995 + (12% over $9,950)
22%	$40,526 to $86,375	$4,664 + (22% over $40,525)
24%	$86,376 to $164,925	$14,751 + (24% over $86,375)
32%	$164,926 to $209,425	$33,603 + (32% over $164,925)
35%	$209,426 to $314,150	$47,843 + (35% over $209,425)
37%	$314,151 or more	$84,496.75 + (37% over $314,150)

FORMS & SCHEDULES OF FORM 1040

Form **1040** Department of the Treasury—Internal Revenue Service (99) **U.S. Individual Income Tax Return** **2021** OMB No. 1545-0074 IRS Use Only—Do not write or staple in this space.

Filing Status ☐ Single ☐ Married filing jointly ☐ Married filing separately (MFS) ☐ Head of household (HOH) ☐ Qualifying widow(er) (QW)
Check only one box.
If you checked the MFS box, enter the name of your spouse. If you checked the HOH or QW box, enter the child's name if the qualifying person is a child but not your dependent ▶

Your first name and middle initial	Last name			**Your social security number**
If joint return, spouse's first name and middle initial	Last name			**Spouse's social security number**
Home address (number and street). If you have a P.O. box, see instructions.			Apt. no.	**Presidential Election Campaign** Check here if you, or your spouse if filing jointly, want $3 to go to this fund. Checking a box below will not change your tax or refund. ☐ You ☐ Spouse
City, town, or post office. If you have a foreign address, also complete spaces below.		State	ZIP code	
Foreign country name	Foreign province/state/county		Foreign postal code	

At any time during 2021, did you receive, sell, exchange, or otherwise dispose of any financial interest in any virtual currency? ☐ **Yes** ☐ **No**

Standard Deduction **Someone can claim:** ☐ You as a dependent ☐ Your spouse as a dependent
☐ Spouse itemizes on a separate return or you were a dual-status alien

Age/Blindness **You:** ☐ Were born before January 2, 1957 ☐ Are blind **Spouse:** ☐ Was born before January 2, 1957 ☐ Is blind

Dependents (see instructions):
If more than four dependents, see instructions and check here ▶ ☐

(1) First name Last name	(2) Social Security number	(3) Relationship to you	✔ if qualifies for (see instructions): Child tax credit	Credit for other dependents
			☐	☐
			☐	☐
			☐	☐
			☐	☐

Attach Sch. B if required.

1	Wages, salaries, tips, etc. Attach Form(s) W-2			1	
2a	Tax-exempt interest	2a	b Taxable interest	2b	
3a	Qualified dividends	3a	b Ordinary dividends	3b	
4a	IRA distributions	4a	b Taxable amount	4b	
5a	Pensions and annuities	5a	b Taxable amount	5b	
6a	Social security benefits	6a	b Taxable amount	6b	
7	Capital gain or (loss). Attach Schedule D if required. If not required, check here ▶ ☐			7	
8	Other income from Schedule 1, line 10			8	
9	Add lines 1, 2b, 3b, 4b, 5b, 6b, 7, and 8. This is your **total income** ▶			9	
10	Adjustments to income from Schedule 1, line 26			10	
11	Subtract line 10 from line 9. This is your **adjusted gross income** ▶			11	
12a	**Standard deduction or itemized deductions** (from Schedule A)	12a			
b	Charitable contributions if you take the standard deduction (see instructions)	12b			
c	Add lines 12a and 12b			12c	
13	Qualified business income deduction from Form 8995 or Form 8995-A			13	
14	Add lines 12c and 13			14	
15	**Taxable income.** Subtract line 14 from line 11. If zero or less, enter -0-			15	

Standard Deduction for—
- Single or Married filing separately, $12,550
- Married filing jointly or Qualifying widow(er), $25,100
- Head of household, $18,800
- If you checked any box under *Standard Deduction*, see instructions.

For Disclosure, Privacy Act, and Paperwork Reduction Act Notice, see separate instructions. Cat. No. 11320B Form **1040** (2021)

Schedule

Form

See Instructions

Form 1040 (2021) Page **2**

	16	**Tax** (see instructions). Check if any from Form(s): **1** ☐ 8814 **2** ☐ 4972 **3** ☐ ______		16	
	17	Amount from Schedule 2, line 3		17	
	18	Add lines 16 and 17		18	
	19	Nonrefundable child tax credit or credit for other dependents from Schedule 8812		19	
	20	Amount from Schedule 3, line 8		20	
	21	Add lines 19 and 20		21	
	22	Subtract line 21 from line 18. If zero or less, enter -0-		22	
	23	Other taxes, including self-employment tax, from Schedule 2, line 21		23	
	24	Add lines 22 and 23. This is your **total tax** ▶		24	
	25	Federal income tax withheld from:			
	a	Form(s) W-2	25a		
	b	Form(s) 1099	25b		
	c	Other forms (see instructions)	25c		
	d	Add lines 25a through 25c		25d	
If you have a qualifying child, attach Sch. EIC.	26	2021 estimated tax payments and amount applied from 2020 return		26	
	27a	Earned income credit (EIC)	27a		
		Check here if you were born after January 1, 1998, and before January 2, 2004, and you satisfy all the other requirements for taxpayers who are at least age 18, to claim the EIC. See instructions ☐			
	b	Nontaxable combat pay election 27b			
	c	Prior year (2019) earned income 27c			
	28	Refundable child tax credit or additional child tax credit from Schedule 8812	28		
	29	American opportunity credit from Form 8863, line 8	29		
	30	Recovery rebate credit. See instructions	30		
	31	Amount from Schedule 3, line 15	31		
	32	Add lines 27a and 28 through 31. These are your **total other payments and refundable credits** ▶		32	
	33	Add lines 25d, 26, and 32. These are your **total payments** ▶		33	
Refund	34	If line 33 is more than line 24, subtract line 24 from line 33. This is the amount you **overpaid**		34	
	35a	Amount of line 34 you want **refunded to you.** If Form 8888 is attached, check here ▶ ☐		35a	
Direct deposit? See instructions.	▶ b	Routing number ▶ **c** Type: ☐ Checking ☐ Savings			
	▶ d	Account number			
	36	Amount of line 34 you want **applied to your 2022 estimated tax** ▶	36		
Amount You Owe	37	**Amount you owe.** Subtract line 33 from line 24. For details on how to pay, see instructions ▶		37	
	38	Estimated tax penalty (see instructions) ▶	38		

Third Party Designee

Do you want to allow another person to discuss this return with the IRS? See instructions ▶ ☐ **Yes.** Complete below. ☐ **No**

Designee's name ▶ | Phone no. ▶ | Personal identification number (PIN) ▶

Sign Here

Under penalties of perjury, I declare that I have examined this return and accompanying schedules and statements, and to the best of my knowledge and belief, they are true, correct, and complete. Declaration of preparer (other than taxpayer) is based on all information of which preparer has any knowledge.

Joint return? See instructions. Keep a copy for your records.

Your signature	Date	Your occupation	If the IRS sent you an Identity Protection PIN, enter it here (see inst.) ▶
Spouse's signature. If a joint return, **both** must sign.	Date	Spouse's occupation	If the IRS sent your spouse an Identity Protection PIN, enter it here (see inst.) ▶
Phone no.	Email address		

Paid Preparer Use Only

Preparer's name	Preparer's signature	Date	PTIN	Check if: ☐ Self-employed
Firm's name ▶			Phone no.	
Firm's address ▶			Firm's EIN ▶	

Go to *www.irs.gov/Form1040* for instructions and the latest information. Form **1040** (2021)

Schedule

Form

See Instructions

Form 1040: US Individual Income Tax Return

Form **1040** Department of the Treasury—Internal Revenue Service (99) **U.S. Individual Income Tax Return** **2021** OMB No. 1545-0074 IRS Use Only—Do not write or staple in this space.

Filing Status Check only one box. ☐ Single ☐ Married filing jointly ☐ Married filing separately (MFS) ☐ Head of household (HOH) ☐ Qualifying widow(er) (QW)

If you checked the MFS box, enter the name of your spouse. If you checked the HOH or QW box, enter the child's name if the qualifying person is a child but not your dependent ►

Your first name and middle initial	Last name			**Your social security number**
If joint return, spouse's first name and middle initial	Last name			**Spouse's social security number**
Home address (number and street). If you have a P.O. box, see instructions.			Apt. no.	**Presidential Election Campaign** Check here if you, or your spouse if filing jointly, want $3 to go to this fund. Checking a box below will not change your tax or refund. ☐ You ☐ Spouse
City, town, or post office. If you have a foreign address, also complete spaces below.		State	ZIP code	
Foreign country name	Foreign province/state/county		Foreign postal code	

At any time during 2021, did you receive, sell, exchange, or otherwise dispose of any financial interest in any virtual currency? ☐ Yes ☐ No

Standard Deduction **Someone can claim:** ☐ You as a dependent ☐ Your spouse as a dependent
☐ Spouse itemizes on a separate return or you were a dual-status alien

Age/Blindness **You:** ☐ Were born before January 2, 1957 ☐ Are blind **Spouse:** ☐ Was born before January 2, 1957 ☐ Is blind

Dependents (see instructions): If more than four dependents, see instructions and check here ► ☐

(1) First name Last name	number	(3) to you	✔ if qualifies for (see instructions): Child tax credit	Credit for other dependents
			☐	☐
			☐	☐
			☐	☐
			☐	☐

Attach Sch. B if required.

1	Wages, salaries, tips, etc. Attach Form(s) W-2			1	
2a	Tax-exempt interest	2a	b Taxable interest	2b	
3a	Qualified dividends	3a	b Ordinary dividends	3b	
4a	IRA distributions	4a	b Taxable amount	4b	
5a	Pensions and annuities	5a	b Taxable amount	5b	
6a	Social security benefits	6a	b Taxable amount	6b	
7	Capital gain or (loss). Attach Schedule D if required. If not required, check here ► ☐			7	
8	Other income from Schedule 1, line 10			8	
9	Add lines 1, 2b, 3b, 4b, 5b, 6b, 7, and 8. This is your **total income** ►			9	
10	Adjustments to income from Schedule 1, line 26			10	
11	Subtract line 10 from line 9. This is your **adjusted gross income** ►			11	
12a	**Standard deduction or itemized deductions** (from Schedule A)	12a			
b	Charitable contributions if you take the standard deduction (see instructions)	12b			
c	Add lines 12a and 12b			12c	
13	Qualified business income deduction from Form 8995 or Form 8995-A			13	
14	Add lines 12c and 13			14	
15	**Taxable income.** Subtract line 14 from line 11. If zero or less, enter -0-			15	

Standard Deduction for—
- Single or Married filing separately, $12,550
- Married filing jointly or Qualifying widow(er), $25,100
- Head of household, $18,800
- If you checked any box under *Standard Deduction*, see instructions.

For Disclosure, Privacy Act, and Paperwork Reduction Act Notice, see separate instructions. Cat. No. 11320B Form **1040** (2021)

Personal Information.
Spell your name(s) as listed on your SS card(s). Provide the address where you are currently living.

The most important number is your Social Security number (SSN). If you have an Individual Taxpayer Identification Number (ITIN), use that on the SSN line.

Virtual Currency.
Mark "Yes" if you sold, exchanged or received virtual currency in 2021. You don't need to check it if you held it or purchased it.

Filing Status & Requirements (2021).

Status	Income Requirement	Extra over per filer > 65
Single (S)	$12,500	$1,700
Head of Household (HOH)	$18,800	$1,700
Married Filing Jointly (MFJ)	$25,100	$1,350
Qualifying Widow(er) (QW)	$25,100	$1,350
Married Filing Separately (MFS)	$5	

HOH and QW statuses require dependents.

Dependents.
List of child and other dependents who qualified for child tax credit (CTC) or credit for other dependents (COD).

Line 1.
Total wages, salaries, tips, including spouse's income from W-2s.

Line 2a & 2b.
Total tax-exempt interest on 1099-INT or 1099-OID, What's taxable (2b).

Line 3a.
Qualified dividends shown in box 1b of 1099-DIV. Eligible for a lower tax rate when held > 60 days for common stocks.

Line 3b.
Ordinary dividends on 1099-DIV, including REITs. Require Such B if total over $1,500.

Line 4a & 4b.
Total IRA distributions on 1099-R from Roth IRA, traditional IRA, SEP, or SIMPLE IRA. What's taxable (4b).

Line 5a & 5b.
Total pensions & annuities on 1099-R. What's taxable (5b).

Line 6a & 6b.
Total social security benefits on SSA-1099 or RRB-1099. What's taxable (6b).

Line 7.
Capital gain/loss after sell of stocks, investments or home on 1099-DIV, Form 8949 or Sch D.

Line 8.
Additional income from Sch 1 Part I.

Line 9.
Total income.

Line 10.
Adjustments to income (deductions) from Sch 1 Part II.

Line 11.
Adjusted gross income (AGI).

Line 12a.
Itemized (Sch A) or standard deduction (SD).
SD for 2021:
S/MFS - $12,550;
HOH - $18,800;
MFJ/QW - $25,100.

Extra deduction for age over 65 or blindness.

Line 12b.
Charitable deductions up to $300 for S, HOH, QW or MFJ, if you don't itemize.

Line 13.
Qualified Business Income Deduction (QBI) worth up to 20% of business income for qualified business on Sch C or rental on Sch E, calculated on Form 8995.

Line 15.
Taxable income.

Form 1040: US Individual Income Tax Return *(cont.)*

Form 1040 (2021) Page **2**

16	**Tax** (see instructions). Check if any from Form(s): 1 ☐ 8814 2 ☐ 4972 3 ☐ ______			16	
17	Amount from Schedule 2, line 3			17	
18	Add lines 16 and 17			18	
19	Nonrefundable child tax credit or credit for other dependents from Schedule 8812			19	
20	Amount from Schedule 3, line 8			20	
21	Add lines 19 and 20			21	
22	Subtract line 21 from line 18. If zero or less, enter -0-			22	
23	Other taxes, including self-employment tax, from Schedule 2, line 21			23	
24	Add lines 22 and 23. This is your **total tax** ▶			24	
25	Federal income tax withheld from:				
a	Form(s) W-2	25a			
b	Form(s) 1099	25b			
c	Other forms (see instructions)	25c			
d	Add lines 25a through 25c			25d	
26	2021 estimated tax payments and amount applied from 2020 return			26	
27a	Earned income credit (EIC)	27a			
	Check here if you were born after January 1, 1998, and before January 2, 2004, and you satisfy all the other requirements for taxpayers who are at least age 18, to claim the EIC. See instructions ☐				
b	Nontaxable combat pay election	27b			
c	Prior year (2019) earned income	27c			
28	Refundable child tax credit or additional child tax credit from Schedule 8812	28			
29	American opportunity credit from Form 8863, line 8	29			
30	Recovery rebate credit. See instructions	30			
31	Amount from Schedule 3, line 15	31			
32	Add lines 27a and 28 through 31. These are your **total other payments and refundable credits** ▶			32	
33	Add lines 25d, 26, and 32. These are your **total payments** ▶			33	

If you have a qualifying child, attach Sch. EIC.

Refund

34	If line 33 is more than line 24, subtract line 24 from line 33. This is the amount you **overpaid**	34	
35a	Amount of line 34 you want **refunded to you.** If Form 8888 is attached, check here ▶ ☐	35a	
▶ b	Routing number ▶ c Type: ☐ Checking ☐ Savings		
▶ d	Account number		
36	Amount of line 34 you want **applied to your 2022 estimated tax** ▶ 36		

Direct deposit? See instructions.

Amount You Owe

37	**Amount you owe.** Subtract line 33 from line 24. For details on how to pay, see instructions ▶	37	
38	Estimated tax penalty (see instructions) ▶ 38		

Third Party Designee

Do you want to allow another person to discuss this return with the IRS? See instructions ▶ ☐ **Yes.** Complete below. ☐ **No**

Designee's name ▶ Phone no. ▶ Personal identification number (PIN) ▶

Sign Here

Under penalties of perjury, I declare that I have examined this return and accompanying schedules and statements, and to the best of my knowledge and belief, they are true, correct, and complete. Declaration of preparer (other than taxpayer) is based on all information of which preparer has any knowledge.

Your signature	Date	Your occupation	If the IRS sent you an Identity Protection PIN, enter it here (see inst.) ▶
Spouse's signature. If a joint return, **both** must sign.	Date	Spouse's occupation	If the IRS sent your spouse an Identity Protection PIN, enter it here (see inst.) ▶
Phone no.	Email address		

Joint return? See instructions. Keep a copy for your records.

Paid Preparer Use Only

Preparer's name	Preparer's signature	Date	PTIN	Check if: ☐ Self-employed
Firm's name ▶			Phone no.	
Firm's address ▶			Firm's EIN ▶	

Go to *www.irs.gov/Form1040* for instructions and the latest information. Form **1040** (2021)

Third Party Designee.
If you want to allow someone else to discuss your tax return with the IRS, check "Yes."

Signature, Date & Identity Protection PIN.
You need to sign & date your tax return in order to be valid. For e-filing, you need to sign with a self-selected PIN. Included Identity Protection PIN (IP PIN), if your identity has been compromised otherwise your tax return will not be accepted.

Line 16.
Include any additional income not reported earlier such as child's interest or lump-sum distribution tax. Calculate tax due for your filing status and income levels shown in tax tables & tax brackets.

Line 17.
Additional tax from Sch 2 Part I.

Line 19.
Nonrefundable child tax credit /credit for other dependents Form 8812.

Line 20.
Additional non-refundable credits from Sch 3 Part I.

Line 23.
Additional taxes including self-employment tax from Sch 2 Part II.

Line 24.
Total tax.

Line 25 a-c.
Federal income tax withheld on Form(s) W-2 (25a), Form(s) 1099 (25b), and other forms such as W-2G (25c).

Line 26.
2021 estimated tax payments & overpayments from prior year.

Line 37.
Amount you owe.

Line 27a.
Earned Income Tax Credit (EITC) for people who have earned income below certain amount. If you were born between 1/1/98 and 1/2/2004 check the box.

Line 27b.
Nontaxable combat pay.

Line 27c.
Earned income from tax year 2020.

Line 28.
Refundable child tax credit (CTC) or additional child tax credit (ACTC) from 8812. Can result in a refund even if no tax due.

Line 29.
Refundable part of the American Opportunity Tax Credit (AOTC) for education.

Line 30.
Recovery Rebate Credit (RRC) for 3rd stimulus payment that was not received. RRC for 1st & 2nd stimulus was reconciled on tax return for 2020.

Line 31.
Additional payments & refundable credits from Sch 3 Part II.

Line 33.
Total payments & credits.

Line 34.
What you **overpaid**.

Line 35.
What do you want to refunded to you (35) & what you want to apply towards next year.

Line 38.
If you owe more than $1,000 you may pay tax penalty.

Paid Preparer Info.
If you pay for tax preparation, the preparer name, PTIN and firm EIN needs to be included.

Schedule 1 (1040): Additional Income & Adjustments to Income

SCHEDULE 1 (Form 1040) — Department of the Treasury, Internal Revenue Service

Additional Income and Adjustments to Income

▶ Attach to Form 1040, 1040-SR, or 1040-NR.
▶ Go to www.irs.gov/Form1040 for instructions and the latest information.

OMB No. 1545-0074 — 2021 — Attachment Sequence No. 01

Name(s) shown on Form 1040, 1040-SR, or 1040-NR — Your social security number

Part I Additional Income

1	Taxable refunds, credits, or offsets of state and local income taxes		1
2a	Alimony received		2a
b	Date of original divorce or separation agreement (see instructions) ▶		
3	Business income or (loss). Attach Schedule C		3
4	Other gains or (losses). Attach Form 4797		4
5	Rental real estate, royalties, partnerships, S corporations, trusts, etc. Attach Schedule E		5
6	Farm income or (loss). Attach Schedule F		6
7	Unemployment compensation		7
8	Other income:		
a	Net operating loss	8a ( )	
b	Gambling income	8b	
c	Cancellation of debt	8c	
d	Foreign earned income exclusion from Form 2555	8d ( )	
e	Taxable Health Savings Account distribution	8e	
f	Alaska Permanent Fund dividends	8f	
g	Jury duty pay	8g	
h	Prizes and awards	8h	
i	Activity not engaged in for profit income	8i	
j	Stock options	8j	
k	Income from the rental of personal property if you engaged in the rental for profit but were not in the business of renting such property	8k	
l	Olympic and Paralympic medals and USOC prize money (see instructions)	8l	
m	Section 951(a) inclusion (see instructions)	8m	
n	Section 951A(a) inclusion (see instructions)	8n	
o	Section 461(l) excess business loss adjustment	8o	
p	Taxable distributions from an ABLE account (see instructions)	8p	
z	Other income. List type and amount ▶	8z	
9	Total other income. Add lines 8a through 8z		9
10	Combine lines 1 through 7 and 9. Enter here and on Form 1040, 1040-SR, or 1040-NR, line 8		10

For Paperwork Reduction Act Notice, see your tax return instructions. — Cat. No. 71479F — Schedule 1 (Form 1040) 2021

Line 1.
Possible taxable refunds if previous year you itemized & deducted SALT.

Line 2a & 2b.
Alimony received for agreements entered before 12/31/2018.

Line 3.
Business income or loss from Sch C.

Line 4.
Other gains/losses from sale/exchange of assets. Form 4797.

Line 5.
Rental, royalties, partnership or S-Corp income/loss on Sch F.

Line 6.
Farm income or loss from Sch F.

Line 7.
Unemployment received on Form 1099-G in box 1.

Line 8a.
Net operating loss (NOL) carried from earlier year.

Line 8b.
Gambling income received on W-2G. Gambling losses can only be deducted if you itemize.

Line 8c.
Cancellation of debt received on Form 1099-C box 2. Some of it may be non-taxable.

Line 8d.
Foreign earned income exclusion on From 2555 ($108,700 in 2021).

Line 8e.
Taxable HSA distributions.

Line 8j.
Exercise of stock options not reported on line 1 of 1040.

Line 8f.
Jury duty pay.

Line 8h.
Prizes & awards.

Line 8i.
Hobby income. Hobby expenses are not deductible.

Schedule 1 (1040) *(cont.)* Deductions

Schedule 1 (Form 1040) 2021 Page 2

Part II Adjustments to Income

11	Educator expenses	11	
12	Certain business expenses of reservists, performing artists, and fee-basis government officials. Attach Form 2106	12	
13	Health savings account deduction. Attach Form 8889	13	
14	Moving expenses for members of the Armed Forces. Attach Form 3903	14	
15	Deductible part of self-employment tax. Attach Schedule SE	15	
16	Self-employed SEP, SIMPLE, and qualified plans	16	
17	Self-employed health insurance deduction	17	
18	Penalty on early withdrawal of savings	18	
19a	Alimony paid	19a	
b	Recipient's SSN ▶		
c	Date of original divorce or separation agreement (see instructions) ▶		
20	IRA deduction	20	
21	Student loan interest deduction	21	
22	Reserved for future use	22	
23	Archer MSA deduction	23	
24	Other adjustments:		
a	Jury duty pay (see instructions)	24a	
b	Deductible expenses related to income reported on line 8k from the rental of personal property engaged in for profit	24b	
c	Nontaxable amount of the value of Olympic and Paralympic medals and USOC prize money reported on line 8l	24c	
d	Reforestation amortization and expenses	24d	
e	Repayment of supplemental unemployment benefits under the Trade Act of 1974	24e	
f	Contributions to section 501(c)(18)(D) pension plans	24f	
g	Contributions by certain chaplains to section 403(b) plans	24g	
h	Attorney fees and court costs for actions involving certain unlawful discrimination claims (see instructions)	24h	
i	Attorney fees and court costs you paid in connection with an award from the IRS for information you provided that helped the IRS detect tax law violations	24i	
j	Housing deduction from Form 2555	24j	
k	Excess deductions of section 67(e) expenses from Schedule K-1 (Form 1041)	24k	
z	Other adjustments. List type and amount ▶	24z	
25	Total other adjustments. Add lines 24a through 24z	25	
26	Add lines 11 through 23 and 25. These are your **adjustments to income**. Enter here and on Form 1040 or 1040-SR, line 10, or Form 1040-NR, line 10a	26	

Schedule 1 (Form 1040) 2021

Line 11.
Educator expenses up to $250 per filer. Requires 900 hrs of teaching.

Line 12.
Business expenses of reservists, performing artists, etc.

Line 13.
HSA deduction up to $3,600 per filer (2021).

Line 14.
Moving expenses only for Armed Forces on active duty.

Line 15.
Half of self-employment tax from Sch SE.

Line 16.
Self-employed SEP, SIMPLE plans.

Line 17.
Self-employed health insurance deduction if you had net profit on Sch C or F, S-Corp or partnership

Line 18.
Penalty on early withdrawal of savings.

Line 19.
Alimony paid for agreements entered before 12/31/2018.

Line 20.
Traditional IRA deduction of up to $6,000 per filer ($7,000 if over 50).

Line 21.
Student loan interest deduction up to $2,500.

Line 24b.
Expenses related to property rental that was not a recurring business activity.

Line 24e.
Repayment of unemployment pay.

Line 24h.
Legal costs in connection with discrimination claims.

Line 24j.
Foreign housing exclusion deduction from Form 2555

Schedule 2 (1040) Additional Taxes

SCHEDULE 2
(Form 1040)
Department of the Treasury
Internal Revenue Service

Additional Taxes

▶ Attach to Form 1040, 1040-SR, or 1040-NR.
▶ Go to www.irs.gov/Form1040 for instructions and the latest information.

OMB No. 1545-0074
2021
Attachment Sequence No. **02**

Name(s) shown on Form 1040, 1040-SR, or 1040-NR | **Your social security number**

Part I Tax

1	Alternative minimum tax. Attach Form 6251	1	
2	Excess advance premium tax credit repayment. Attach Form 8962	2	
3	Add lines 1 and 2. Enter here and on Form 1040, 1040-SR, or 1040-NR, line 17	3	

Part II Other Taxes

4	Self-employment tax. Attach Schedule SE	4	
5	Social security and Medicare tax on unreported tip income. Attach Form 4137	5	
6	Uncollected social security and Medicare tax on wages. Attach Form 8919	6	
7	Total additional social security and Medicare tax. Add lines 5 and 6	7	
8	Additional tax on IRAs or other tax-favored accounts. Attach Form 5329 if required	8	
9	Household employment taxes. Attach Schedule H	9	
10	Repayment of first-time homebuyer credit. Attach Form 5405 if required	10	
11	Additional Medicare Tax. Attach Form 8959	11	
12	Net investment income tax. Attach Form 8960	12	
13	Uncollected social security and Medicare or RRTA tax on tips or group-term life insurance from Form W-2, box 12	13	
14	Interest on tax due on installment income from the sale of certain residential lots and timeshares	14	
15	Interest on the deferred tax on gain from certain installment sales with a sales price over $150,000	15	
16	Recapture of low-income housing credit. Attach Form 8611	16	

(continued on page 2)

For Paperwork Reduction Act Notice, see your tax return instructions. Cat. No. 71478U Schedule 2 (Form 1040) 2021

Line 1. Alternative Minimum Tax (AMT). Exemption of $73,600 for single & $114,600 for MFJ.

Line 2. Amount of advanced premium tax credit (APTC) repayment for excess in subsidies received for Marketplace health insurance. Form 1095-A.

Line 4. Self-employment tax from Sch SE.

Line 5. SS and Medicare tax on tips not reported to an employer.

Line 6. SS and Medicare tax not collected on wages.

Line 8. Additional tax on IRAs, etc. such as excess contributions or early withdrawals.

Line 9. Employment taxes for household employees such as nannies, health aids, on Sch H. If paid more than $2,300 in 2021.

Line 10. First-time homebuyer credit repayment from 2008 through 2010. Check account status at https://sa.www4.irs.gov/irfof-fthb/login.

Line 11. Additional Medicare tax for taxpayers making $200,000 (S), $250,000 (MFJ).

Line 12. Net investment tax of 3.8% on dividends, taxable interest, rents, royalties, etc., if MAGI of $200,000 (S) or $250,000 (MFJ).

Line 14 & 15. Interest on tax due or deferred tax on installment sales.

Line 16. Recapture of low-income housing credit b/u of disposal, or failure in procedure, etc.

Schedule 2 (1040) *(cont.)* Other Taxes

Schedule 2 (Form 1040) 2021 Page **2**

Part II **Other Taxes** *(continued)*

17	Other additional taxes:		
a	Recapture of other credits. List type, form number, and amount ▶	17a	
b	Recapture of federal mortgage subsidy. If you sold your home in 2021, see instructions	17b	
c	Additional tax on HSA distributions. Attach Form 8889	17c	
d	Additional tax on an HSA because you didn't remain an eligible individual. Attach Form 8889	17d	
e	Additional tax on Archer MSA distributions. Attach Form 8853	17e	
f	Additional tax on Medicare Advantage MSA distributions. Attach Form 8853	17f	
g	Recapture of a charitable contribution deduction related to a fractional interest in tangible personal property	17g	
h	Income you received from a nonqualified deferred compensation plan that fails to meet the requirements of section 409A	17h	
i	Compensation you received from a nonqualified deferred compensation plan described in section 457A	17i	
j	Section 72(m)(5) excess benefits tax	17j	
k	Golden parachute payments	17k	
l	Tax on accumulation distribution of trusts	17l	
m	Excise tax on insider stock compensation from an expatriated corporation	17m	
n	Look-back interest under section 167(g) or 460(b) from Form 8697 or 8866	17n	
o	Tax on non-effectively connected income for any part of the year you were a nonresident alien from Form 1040-NR	17o	
p	Any interest from Form 8621, line 16f, relating to distributions from, and dispositions of, stock of a section 1291 fund	17p	
q	Any interest from Form 8621, line 24	17q	
z	Any other taxes. List type and amount ▶	17z	
18	Total additional taxes. Add lines 17a through 17z		18
19	Additional tax from Schedule 8812		19
20	Section 965 net tax liability installment from Form 965-A	20	
21	Add lines 4, 7 through 16, 18, and 19. These are your **total other taxes.** Enter here and on Form 1040 or 1040-SR, line 23, or Form 1040-NR, line 23b		21

Schedule 2 (Form 1040) 2021

Line 17a.
Recapture of credits such as investment credit, Indian employment credit, alternative motor vehicle credit, etc.

Line 17c.
Additional tax on unqualified HSA distributions.

Line 17e.
Additional tax on unqualified Archer MSA distributions.

Line 17g.
Additional tax on recapture of a charitable contribution deduction relating to tangible personal property.

Line 17h.
Additional tax on income received from non qualified deferred compensation plan.

Line 17l.
Additional tax on accumulation distribution of trust.

Line 17k.
Additional tax of 20% on excess parachute payment (EPP) shown on Form W-2 Box 12 with code K or 1099-MISC Box 13. EPP apply to highly compensated individuals and 1% shareholders of a C-Corp.

Line 17m.
Additional tax on insider stock compensation from an expatriated corp.

Line 17o.
Any tax on non effectively connected income for any part of the year you were a nonresident alien and filed 1040-NR.

Line 17q.
Any interest for a shareholder of a passive foreign investment company or qualified electing fund on Form 8621 line 24.

Schedule 3 (1040) Non-refundable Credits

SCHEDULE 3
(Form 1040)
Department of the Treasury
Internal Revenue Service

Additional Credits and Payments
▶ Attach to Form 1040, 1040-SR, or 1040-NR.
▶ Go to www.irs.gov/Form1040 for instructions and the latest information.

OMB No. 1545-0074
2021
Attachment Sequence No. 03

Name(s) shown on Form 1040, 1040-SR, or 1040-NR | **Your social security number**

Part I **Nonrefundable Credits**

1	Foreign tax credit. Attach Form 1116 if required		1
2	Credit for child and dependent care expenses from Form 2441, line 11. Attach Form 2441		2
3	Education credits from Form 8863, line 19		3
4	Retirement savings contributions credit. Attach Form 8880		4
5	Residential energy credits. Attach Form 5695		5
6	Other nonrefundable credits:		
a	General business credit. Attach Form 3800	6a	
b	Credit for prior year minimum tax. Attach Form 8801	6b	
c	Adoption credit. Attach Form 8839	6c	
d	Credit for the elderly or disabled. Attach Schedule R	6d	
e	Alternative motor vehicle credit. Attach Form 8910	6e	
f	Qualified plug-in motor vehicle credit. Attach Form 8936	6f	
g	Mortgage interest credit. Attach Form 8396	6g	
h	District of Columbia first-time homebuyer credit. Attach Form 8859	6h	
i	Qualified electric vehicle credit. Attach Form 8834	6i	
j	Alternative fuel vehicle refueling property credit. Attach Form 8911	6j	
k	Credit to holders of tax credit bonds. Attach Form 8912	6k	
l	Amount on Form 8978, line 14. See instructions	6l	
z	Other nonrefundable credits. List type and amount ▶	6z	
7	Total other nonrefundable credits. Add lines 6a through 6z		7
8	Add lines 1 through 5 and 7. Enter here and on Form 1040, 1040-SR, or 1040-NR, line 20		8

(continued on page 2)

For Paperwork Reduction Act Notice, see your tax return instructions. Cat. No. 71480G **Schedule 3 (Form 1040) 2021**

Line 1.
Foreign tax credit from Form 1116 or Form 1099-DIV, 1099-INT, Sch K.

Line 2.
Credit for child & dependent care expenses for children under 13 or disabled dependent. Form 2441.

Line 3.
Education credit from Form 8862. Non-refundable AOTC or LLC.

Line 4.
Saver's credit for retirement contributions to 401(k) or 403(b), etc., if AGI less than $33,000 (S) or $66,000 (MFJ).

Line 5.
Residential energy credits for qualified solar electric, solar water, etc. property.

Line 6a.
Business credit for partners or shareholders in S-corp, self-employed or rental owners.

Line 6c.
Adoption credit up to $14,440 (2021) for expenses. Income limit thresholds apply.

Line 6d.
Credit for the elderly or disabled b/w $3,750 and $7,500. 15% of expenses for taxpayers with AGI of $17,500 (S / HOH / QW) or $20,000 (MFJ) on Sch R.

Line 6f.
Qualified plug-in electric drive motor vehicle credit on Form 8936 from $2,500 to $7,500.

Line 6g.
Mortgage interest credit if received a mortgage credit certificate from state or local government. Form 8396.

Schedule 3 (1040) *(cont.)* Payments & Refundable Credits

Schedule 3 (Form 1040) 2021 — Page 2

Part II Other Payments and Refundable Credits

9	Net premium tax credit. Attach Form 8962		9
10	Amount paid with request for extension to file (see instructions)		10
11	Excess social security and tier 1 RRTA tax withheld		11
12	Credit for federal tax on fuels. Attach Form 4136		12
13	Other payments or refundable credits:		
a	Form 2439	13a	
b	Qualified sick and family leave credits from Schedule(s) H and Form(s) 7202 for leave taken before April 1, 2021	13b	
c	Health coverage tax credit from Form 8885	13c	
d	Credit for repayment of amounts included in income from earlier years	13d	
e	Reserved for future use	13e	
f	Deferred amount of net 965 tax liability (see instructions)	13f	
g	Credit for child and dependent care expenses from Form 2441, line 10. Attach Form 2441	13g	
h	Qualified sick and family leave credits from Schedule(s) H and Form(s) 7202 for leave taken after March 31, 2021	13h	
z	Other payments or refundable credits. List type and amount ▶ ______	13z	
14	Total other payments or refundable credits. Add lines 13a through 13z		14
15	Add lines 9 through 12 and 14. Enter here and on Form 1040, 1040-SR, or 1040-NR, line 31		15

Schedule 3 (Form 1040) 2021

Line 9.
Net premium tax credit for taxpayers with Marketplace insurance if they qualified for higher subsidies. Form 1095-A.

Line 10.
Amount of payment made with the 6-mo extension to file (Form 4868).

Line 11.
Excess of SS withheld for taxpayers with wages over $142,800. Excess over $8,853.60 for 2021.

Line 13a.
Undistributed long-term capital gains to shareholders on Form 2439.

Line 13b.
Qualified sick & family leave credits taken before April 1, 2021. From Sch H for household employment taxes or Form 7202 if you were self-employed. Can be up to max of $511 per day or $5,110 in total for sick pay and $200 per day or $12,000 in total for family leave pay.

Line 13d.
Credit for repayment of income claimed in previous year.

Line 13g.
Refundable part of the credit for child and dependent care expenses for children under 13 or disabled dependents up to $4,000 for one and $8,000 for two or more qualified persons. Up to 50% of expenses paid for AGI below $125,000, which falls to 20% for AGI above that and below $183,001 for 2021. No credit for AGI above $400,000.

Line 13h.
Same as line 13b for qualified sick & family leave credits taken after March 31, 2021.

Taxable and Non-Taxable Income[97]

Taxable Income	Non-taxable Income
• Alimony (for divorce before 12/31/2018) • Business income • Canceled debts • Cash income • Compensation for personal services • Director's fees • Disability benefits (employer-funded) • Dividends • Estate and trust income • Farm income • Gains from sale of property or securities • Gambling winnings • Hobby income Interest • Interest • Jury duty fees • Military pay (not exempt from taxation) • Military pension • Non-employee compensation • Partnership, Estate and S-Corporation income (Schedule K-1s, Taxpayer's share) • Pensions • Prizes • Punitive damage award	• Aid to Families with Dependent Children (AFDC) • Alimony received for court orders after 12/31/2018 • Child support • Civil damages, restitution for wrongful incarceration • Damages for physical injury (other than punitive) • Death payments • Dividends on life insurance • Economic Impact Payment (EIPs), Stimulus Payments • Employee education assistance from an employer up to $5,250 • Employer reimbursements for ordinary or necessary expenses • Federal income tax refunds • Foreign earned income up to $108,500 (2021) • Gifts • Home sale exclusion on primary residence up to $250,000 per filer • Inheritance or bequest • Insurance proceeds (Accident, Casualty, Health, Life) • Interest on EE/I bonds redeemed for qualified higher education expenses • Interest on tax-free securities

97 *https://apps.irs.gov/app/vita/content/globalmedia/teacher/examples_of_taxable_nontaxable_income.pdf*

Taxable Income

- Railroad retirement
- Refunds of State and local income tax (if reportable)
- Rent income
- Rewards
- Royalties
- Self-employment income
- Severance pay
- Social security benefits - portion may be taxable -
- Taxable scholarships and grants
- Tips and gratuities
- Unemployment compensation
- Wages, salaries, bonuses, commissions

Non-taxable Income

- Meals and lodging for the convenience of employer
- Olympic & Paralympic medals and prizes
- Payments to the beneficiary of a deceased employee
- Qualified Medicaid waiver payments
- Relocation payments
- Rental allowance of clergyman
- Rental income for less than 15 days
- Repayments of excess Advanced Premium Tax Credit for marketplace insurance subsidies suspended *(Tax Year 2020 only)*
- Reverse mortgages
- Sickness and injury payments
- Social security benefits - portion may not be taxable
- Supplemental Security Income (SSI)
- Temporary Assistance for Needy Families (TANF)
- Unemployment compensation up to $10,200 per filer *(Tax Year 2020 only)*
- Veterans' benefits
- Welfare payments & food stamps
- Worker's compensation

Glossary

A	**Ability to Pay**	Basis of a progressive tax system, where taxpayers with higher income pay more in taxes than those with lower incomes.
	Above-the-line Deduction	Also called adjustment to income. Deductions that tax breaks that taxpayers can take to reduce their gross income without having to itemize.
	Adjusted (Cost) Basis	It is used to determine the loss or gain on a sale of property. The formula used is: (original cost of property + value of improvements + any fees & expenses) - depreciation = adjusted basis.
	Adjusted Gross Income (AGI)	It is your gross income from your wages, dividends, capital gains, business income, retirement distributions, and other income, less certain adjustments listed on Schedule 1 Part II. AGI is an important item as it is often referenced in calculating deductions or credits and as an identity verification item in tax software.
	Alternative Minimum Tax (AMT)	A special tax system that was originally intended to prevent wealthy taxpayers from taking advantage of so many tax-breaks that they ended up paying little or no taxes.
	Amended Return	A return that is filed to make corrections on the originally filed return.
	American Opportunity Tax Credit (AOTC)	It is a partially refundable tax credit available to taxpayers within the first four years of post-secondary education to offset the cost of qualified expenses. The maximum annual credit per student is $2,500.
	Annuity	It is a fixed sum of money paid to a person annually, such as from a retirement plan.
	Audit	An IRS review or an examination of a tax return. It can be selected at random or be based on a number of red flags.
B	**Bad Debt**	It is a debt that tis unlikely to be paid.
	Brackets	*See Tax Brackets.*

C

Cancelled Debt	Forgiven or discharged debts that are often taxable, although some can be non-taxable (e.g., bankruptcy debt, insolvency). See Taxable vs. Non-Taxable Income table.
Capital Gain	The profit made on the sale of property such as stocks, mutual funds and real estate. Gains on assets held less than 12 months are considered short-term capital gains and are taxed at the taxpayer's top tax bracket as any ordinary income. Gains on assets held more than 12 months are considered long-term capital gains and are taxed at a preferential tax rate of either 0%, 15%, or 20%. There are some exceptions for things such as collectible assets such as precious metals and antiques, are taxed at 28%.
Carryover	A process by which a deduction or credit that can't be taken during the year can be applied against a tax liability in subsequent years (Carryforward) or previous years (Carryback).
Charitable Deduction	Deductions allowed for money or property gifts to charity.
Child Support	Payments made to an ex-spouse or legally separated spouse for the care of a child. Child support payments are neither taxable nor deductible.
Credit	*See Tax Credit.*

D

Deduction	*See Tax Deduction.*
Dependents	**Dependents** is someone you support and you can claim on tax return. Generally, when you can claim a dependent you are eligible for additional deductions and credits such as CTC or credit for other dependents. Your filing status can change and your standard deduction is also higher.
Depreciation	An accounting technique in which the cost of an asset is allocated over its useful life and can be deducted as an expense.
Direct Deposit	A method where a tax refund or payment is electronically deposited into a taxpayer's bank account. It is often the fastest and most secure way to receive tax refund.

E

Dividend Profits distributed by corporations to its shareholders in the form of cash, additional shares of stock or other property. All dividends are taxable but qualified dividends are taxed at the lower capital gains tax rate.

Earned Income Compensation earned through a paycheck, self-employment, including wages, salaries and tips. It is derived for providing personal services in employment, trade or business. It requires taxpayer to actually do something for the money.

Effective Tax Rate A rate at which taxpayers would be taxed if their tax liability was taxed at a constant rate rather than progressively. It is calculated by taking the total tax liability for the year and dividing it by total taxable income.

Electronic Filing (E-File) The transmission of tax information directly to the IRS using a computer. It can be done via online software,, when using tax professionals or at a volunteer site.

Employer Identification Number (EIN) It is a 9 digit number to identify business entities.

Estimated Tax **Estimated Tax** is the quarterly payment that a taxpayer may need to pay to the IRS in order to avoid the underpayment penalty if they owe more than $1,000 at the end of the tax year. If you have income not subject to withholdings, such as self-employment or investments, you may need to make quarterly payments. The due dates for estimated payments are: April 15, June 15, September 15, and January 15 of the following year.

Examination *See Audit.*

Exclusions Indicates income that is exempt, or not included, in the calculation of gross income for tax purposes.

Exemption *See Tax Exemption.*

Extension Taxpayers may request a 6-month extension to file their tax returns by submitting Form 4868, Application for Automatic Extension of Time to File US Individual Tax Return. It moves the typical April 15 filing deadline to October 15. The extension to file does not extend the amount of time to pay.

F

Filing Status | One of five tax ranks determined by your martial status, your dependents and how you file. Taxpayers can file as: Single (S), Married Filing Jointly (MFJ), Married Filing Separately (MFS), Head of Household (HOH), or Qualified Widow(er) (QW). The tax rate used to tax taxpayer's income is based on their filing status.

G

Gross Income | Total income from taxable sources before any adjustments, exemptions, credits and deductions are subtracted.

H

Head of Household (HOH) | A filing status claimed by taxpayers who are single or married but can be considered unmarried and who had qualifying dependents, who lived with them and for whom they provided more than half the cost of keeping up the home.

Health Savings Account (HSA) | A special tax-favored account for savings to cover current and future health care expenses.

Hobby | An activity pursued not primarily for financial gain but for enjoyment, sport or entertainment.

Household Employee | A person that is paid to cook, clean, care for dependents of the taxpayer.

I

Identity Protection PIN (IP PIN) | It is a six-digit code assigned to taxpayers who have been victims of identity theft.

Income Taxes | Taxes paid by taxpayers and businesses base don earned and unearned income.

Individual Retirement Account (IRA) | A personal savings account that allows taxpayers to set aside money for retirement. There can be certain benefits for making IRA contributions or distributions, depending on the type of IRA.

Individual Taxpayer Identification Number (ITIN) | **ITIN** means Individual Taxpayer identification number. It is 9 digit long and start with 9. It is assigned to taxpayers who are ineligible to obtain SSN.

Interest Income | The income a taxpayer receives from lending their money or investments, such as savings accounts or CDs.

Internal Revenue Service (IRS) | A bureau of the Department of the Treasury, the IRS is the government agency responsible for collecting taxes and for enforcing the tax code.

	Investment Income	Income derived from the investment of capital, whether money or property, in income-producing assets or profit-making venture, without active participation, such as interest, dividends, capital gains net income, certain rents and royalty, etc.
	Itemized Deduction	It is the amount you can subtract from your gross income to calculate taxable income, that requires support and records for the items listed on Schedule A. It is an alternative to standard deduction for some taxpayers that have large mortgage interest, real estate taxes, state and local taxes or sales taxes, and other items.
J	**Joint Return**	One return filled jointly by two married taxpayers.
L	**Long-Term Capital Gains**	Gains on assets held more than 12 months are considered long-term capital gains and are taxed at a preferential tax rate of either 0%, 15%, or 20%
	Losses	A term defining expenses exceeding revenues.
M	**Marginal Tax Rate**	It is how much of each additional dollar of income that taxpayer makes, will be taxed. It is the top bracket for taxpayer's income. For 2021, if you are single and your AGI is $45,000, you are in the 22% bracket so your marginal tax rate is 22%.
	Medicare Tax	Payroll tax collected from taxpayers to fund medical benefits for people who retire and are over 65.
N	**Non-Refundable Credit**	Tax credits that can reduce your tax liability to zero amount due and any excess is lost.
	Non-Resident	A taxpayer that did not live in particular state but worked or did business there and therefore must file a state income tax return.
	Non-Taxable	Income which is not subject to tax.
P	**Passive Income**	Income received from an activity where the taxpayer doesn't have to actively participate, such as dividends, interest, rental income, royalties, etc.
	Passthrough Entities	Sometimes also called flow-though entities, are businesses whose income flows through onto the 1040 individual form and is taxed under the individual income tax.
	Payroll Tax	Also called Employment Tax. Refers to the Social Security and Medicare taxes that an employer withholds from an employee's paycheck and pays to the government.

	Pension	An employer-sponsored retirement plan that provides a specified payment amount when the taxpayer retires.
	Personal Exemptions	See Tax Exemption.
	Power of Attorney (POA)	Written authorization for a person to receive confidential information from the IRS, as well as perform certain actions, on behalf of a taxpayer. See Section XX.
	Pre-Tax Money	Money that is not subject to tax. Pre-tax money comes out of your paycheck before taxes are calculated. It is not considered part of your gross income.401(k) plans are examples of pre-tax accounts.
	Progressive Taxation	Taxation that has a different tax rate for income in higher income ranges. Taxpayers at lower income levers are taxed at lower tax rate than taxpayers in higher income levels.
	Property Tax	Taxes on property such as real estate, auto or boat.
Q	**Qualifying Child**	To be a qualifying child, the dependent must meet eight tests: (1) relationship, (2) age, (3) residence, (4) support, (5) citizenship or residency, (6) joint return, (7) qualifying child of more than one person, and (8) dependent taxpayer.
	Qualifying Widow(er) (QW)	A filing status that a taxpayer can claim for up to 2 years after passing of their spouse and if: (1) they filed MFJ for the year of death; (2) taxpayer didn't remarry; (3) taxpayer has a qualifying dependent; and (4) the taxpayer provides more than 50% of the cost to maintain the home for the year.
R	**Refund**	The amount of money taxpayer receives back from the IRS if the person paid more in taxes than they owed.
	Refundable (Tax) Credits	Tax credits that bring you up to a refund when you have no tax liability.
	Resident	A taxpayer that lives in a particular state or country.
	Royalties	Payments received for the use of intellectual property such as copyright, patent, trademark, design, etc.
S	**Schedules**	IRS forms that are used to report and calculate various kind of income, deduction and credits.

Scholarship Money awarded for education use. If they are used for qualified educational expenses, they are typically non-taxable.

Self-Employed A taxpayer who works for themselves and are not employees. They can be independent contractors. See Section XX.

Social Security Number (SSN) **SSN** means social security number.

Social Security Tax Payroll benefits for retired and disabled taxpayers and their dependents.

Standard Deduction It is an amount of deduction that varies by filing status, age, blindness and dependency. It reduces taxpayers' income that is subject to tax that does not require specific support. See Table 11.

Statute of Limitations A period within which a specific legal action may take place such as collection of tax, audit, etc.

T

Tax Brackets A range of income taxed at a specific tax rate. There are different tax brackets for different filling statuses. For example, for 2021, the income below $9,950 is taxed at 10% for a single taxpayer and income between $9,950 to $40,525 is taxed at 12%.

Tax Break Use of deductions, credits and exemptions to legally reduce taxes.

Tax Compliance A degree to which taxpayer complies with tax rules and regulations.

Tax Credits It is an amount of money you can subtract, dollar-for-dollar, from the amount of tax you owe, granted that you qualify for the credit by meeting eligibility criteria. Tax credits are better than deductions as a $1,000 of tax credit, reduces your tax liability by exactly $1,000

Tax Cuts and Jobs Act (TCJA) Tax law passed in 2017 and enacted in 2018. It changed deductions, tax rates, credits and other tax items that affect individuals and businesses.Main changes, included: (1) elimination of exemptions; (2) increase in standard deductions; (3) changed itemized deductions; (4) increase of child tax credit; plus number of other changes.

Tax Deduction It is an amount that can be subtracted from your income before you calculate taxable income and tax due. One of the largest tax deduction is the standard or itemized deduction.

	Tax Exemption	It is an amount that is available as a deduction for each qualifying taxpayer or dependent on the tax return. For Federal purposes, all tax exemption have been eliminated since the passing for TCJA law in 2018. Many state tax returns still use exemptions.
	Tax Forms	IRS forms used to report financial information to the agency.
	Tax Liability	The amount of taxes a taxpayer must pay.
	Tax Rates	The percentage rate that is used to tax income for taxpayers and businesses. For example, the federal tax rates on individuals for 2021 are: 10%, 12%, 22%, 24%, 32%, 37%. See the ***Tax Brackets for 2021*.**
	Tax Worksheet	An IRS document that is used to make calculations or determine eligibility for deductions and credits. It is usually not filed with tax returns.
	Tax Year	The 12-month period covered on a tax return that runs from Jan 1 until Dec 31.
	Tax-Exempt Interest Income	Interest income that is not subject to income tax, such as interest earned from municipal bonds.
	Tax-Free Income	Any type of income that you don't have to pay taxes on can, such as child support payments; combat pay; gifts; certain disability payments, etc. See the Taxable and Non-Taxable Income in Appendix.
	Taxable Income	Amount of income used to calculate tax liability. It is AGI, minus deductions and exemptions.
	Taxpayer Identification Number (TIN)	A 9 digit long number that identifies business entities. Also refers to as EIN.
	Tip Income	Money and goods received for services performed that go beyond the stated amount of the bill.
U	**Unearned Income**	Income which is not earned by working, such as investment income, passive holdings, gifts or unemployment.
W	**Withholdings**	The amount of money that is taken out from each paycheck to pay your income, Social Security and Medicare tax. US has a pay-as-you-earn tax system, which means that taxpayers have to pay taxes through withholding with each paycheck.

INDEX

ABOUT THE AUTHOR

I love simplifying and clarifying complex tax information into accessible content. I have a **BA in Economics**, and I am an **IRS Enrolled Agent.**[98] As an Enrolled Agent, I specialize in tax return preparation. I have worked at large tax preparation companies as **Master Tax Advisor** and **Tax Expert**.

Since 2016, I have also volunteered with two **IRS Free Filing programs**. With the **IRS Volunteer Income Tax Assistance (VITA)**,[99] through the Ladder-UP Tax Assistance Program (TAP),[100] I have been preparing tax returns for taxpayers in disadvantaged communities,

With the **Tax Counseling for the Elderly (TCE)**, I have been preparing tax returns for the elderly through the AARP Foundation Tax-Aide.[101]

Connect with me on social media @ https://linktr.ee/akistepinska or at akistepinska@taxguide101.com or on my website www.akistepinska.com

[98] *https://www.irs.gov/tax-professionals/enrolled-agents/enrolled-agent-information*
[99] *https://www.irs.gov/individuals/free-tax-return-preparation-for-qualifying-taxpayers*
[100] *https://www.goladderup.org/our-services/tax-assistance/*
[101] *https://www.aarp.org/money/taxes/aarp_taxaide/*

Made in the USA
Monee, IL
04 November 2026

67377404R00079